T0235453

Computer Supported Cooperative Work

Series Editor:
Richard Harper
Cambridge, United Kingdom

The CSCW series examines the dynamic interface of human nature, culture, and technology. Technology to support groups, once largely confined to workplaces, today affects all aspects of life. Analyses of "Collaboration, Sociality, Computation, and the Web" draw on social, computer and information sciences, aesthetics, and values. Each volume in the series provides a perspective on current knowledge and discussion for one topic, in monographs, edited collections, and textbooks appropriate for those studying, designing, or engaging with sociotechnical systems and artifacts.

Titles published within the Computer Supported Cooperative Work series are included within Thomson Reuters' Book Citation Index.

More information about this series at http://www.springer.com/series/2861

Tone Bratteteig • Ina Wagner

Disentangling Participation

Power and Decision-Making
in Participatory Design

 Springer

Tone Bratteteig
University of Oslo
Department of Informatics
Oslo
Norway

Ina Wagner
University of Oslo
Department of Informatics
Oslo
Norway

ISSN 1431-1496
ISBN 978-3-319-38080-3   ISBN 978-3-319-06163-4 (eBook)
DOI 10.1007/978-3-319-06163-4
Springer Cham Heidelberg New York Dordrecht London

Printed on acid-free paper

Springer is part of Springer Science+Business Media (www.springer.com)

Preface

We have followed participatory design since it's beginning as a political protest movement, seeing it change and diversify over the years. Participatory Design—PD for short—is still around and is being used in a lot of settings that were difficult to imagine in the 1970ies. Participation of users has become important not only in design of IT but also in areas like health care, community development and urban planning. The concept has been stretched as some of the participatory methods were imported and adopted in ways that conflicted with the strong normative roots of PD, i.e., designers sharing power with users and having them influence the design result. In contrast to the 1970ies, the politics of PD has moved to the background. The focus today is more on how to do it than on why.

PD has come to mean a lot of different things to different people, opening up for a range of interpretations, from just any contact with users to emphasizing the moral basis. We found that a closer look at the elements of PD, participation and design, would help us understand: What does it mean to participate? What is it that you participate in in design? This book is our exploration of these questions.

Several people have contributed to strengthening the arguments we build in this book through both, criticism and suggestions for change. We thank Sisse Finken, Kjeld Schmidt, Lucy Suchman, Maja van den Velden, and Guri Verne. We also thank Cornelia Ruland for providing more detailed information about the *Sisom* project; and the *IPCity* team in Vienna and Paris for their reflections and critical discussion of the *IPCity* project.

Contents

Chapter 1
Introduction

Participatory design as an approach to the design of computer-based systems and artifacts aims at involving prospective users in the design process. The participatory design (PD) approach differs from other user or human-centred design approaches by its emphasis on users as co-designers during all stages of the design process, not only as information sources for designers' ideas or testers of more or less finished design results. Users contribute with expert knowledge of the context of which the new technology will become a part and they may ease the process of introducing the technology and putting it to use. A third reason for involving users in design is to enable them to influence the design and have a say on how their future activities with the new technical solution will be (Bjerknes and Bratteteig 1995; Bjørn-Andersen and Hedberg 1977).

> [T]he core principle of PD is that people have a basic right to make decisions about how they do their work and indeed any other activities where they might use technology. This is also the most contested aspect of PD, its most directly stated ethical commitment and its main point of difference to more mainstream user- or human-centred design approaches. (Robertson and Wagner 2012, p. 65)

These core principles have been developed, put into practice and reflected on by many scholars since the early days of PD. The initial Scandinavian PD projects explored how designers could work with users in participatory ways (Bjerknes et al. 1987; Briefs et al. 1983; Clement and Besselaar 1993; Doherty et al. 1987) based on a political agenda of societal change (Bermann 1985; Nygaard 1979; Thorsrud et al. 1976). The early work aimed at arriving at methods and principles for doing PD (Greenbaum and Kyng 1991; Pape and Thoresen 1992). These efforts were important for making PD an integral part of the development of IT (Andersen et al. 1990). Since the early days PD has travelled across continents (Greenbaum 1993; Mathiassen 1997; Schuler and Namioka 1993; Simonsen and Robertson 2012; Floyd et al. 1989; Mambrey et al. 1998; Muller 1993; Robertson 1998) and a myriad of PD methods have been developed (Bødker et al. 2004; Brandt et al. 2012; Bratteteig et al. 2012; Kensing 2003). We also should mention that the multidisciplinarity of PD, e.g. inclusion of thorough ethnographic studies, has long roots in PD (Bermann und Thoresen 1988; Blomberg et al. 1993; Hughes et al. 1992; Nygaard and Sørgård 1987; Suchman 1995; Wynn 1991). PD is a rather practical research area,

T. Bratteig, I. Wagner, *Disentangling Participation,* Computer Supported
Cooperative Work, DOI 10.1007/978-3-319-06163-4_1,
© Springer International Publishing Switzerland 2014

but we also find conceptual and theoretical research that has contributed to the field (e.g.,Bjerknes and Bratteteig 1995; Ehn 1989; Gärtner and Wagner 1996; Robertson 2006; Robertson and Wagner 2012; Wagner 1993). This book aims to contribute to the theoretical perspectives in PD.

Much of the PD literature today explores and provides guidance on how to enrol (prospective) users as co-designers: how to find users and user representatives, how to organize the design process, how to develop a common ground and mutually learn from each other, how to develop ideas and evaluate them as a multidisciplinary team, etc. (Simonsen and Robertson 2012). The most difficult part, however, is the sharing of power inherent in the PD approach: in order to collaborate with users as co-designers the designers need to share their power with them and acknowledge their different and equally valuable expertise. One of the founders of PD, Kristen Nygaard, emphasized the importance for designers to respect users' decisions even if they disagree. This is a strong imperative. What follows from it is a strong commitment to including users in design decisions in all phases of a design project.

This book explores exactly this challenge for practitioners of PD by asking what participation really means: who should participate and in which parts of a design process; what does it mean to share power with users; how are decisions to be made in a participatory way?

In the early days of PD, it was clear that following the 'core principle' of involving users in decisions in all phases of a design process unavoidably led to explicitly addressing issues of politics and power. Hence, dealing with different views and possible conflicts between the stakeholders in a PD project was seen as a part of the process (Ehn and Sandberg 1979). This insight has been somewhat lost in the assumption that 'working with users' almost inevitably would lead designers to do the right thing. A 'modern' version of PD would result in computer-based systems or artifacts that 'appeal both to users and to those who pay' says Kyng, claiming that 'we need to deconstruct the current discussions on "politics" and find new practical ways to cater for the PD aspects of ICT design, including user interests' (Kyng 2010, p. 50). In a commentary Shapiro reflects on what might happen if participatory designers give up on 'politics':

> The most painful question is whether the incorporation of PD into the mainstream of academic and commercial practice has gone so far as actually to make its relationship to users quite exploitative and nakedly instrumental, and to make our repeated claims about the centrality of continuously involving users quite rhetorical and hypocritical. This dismaying revelation is actually quite credible, and should cause many of us to reflect critically on what we do. (Shapiro 2010, p. 73)

The danger of using PD rhetorically for disguising 'quite exploitative and nakedly instrumental' user relationships is one of the motivations for this book. Maybe PD has for many years neglected the politics of design. One exception is Eevi Beck who argues that: 'Rather than participation, concern with power and dominance needs to be stated as the core of the research field of PD' (Beck 2002, p. 77).

Our starting point is the original core of PD: participatory designers are committed to sharing power with users and facilitate a design process where users are able to take part in all phases of a design project. Users' voice should have space and weight. Addressing power issues in PD is therefore critical to having a realistic view onto the possibilities and limitations of participation. We will argue that good intentions on the side of participatory designers are not sufficient, if not paired with cultural sensitivity, a strong sense of responsibility and political insight. Designers have to learn how to use their power and how to share it.

Our motivation for this book is what we perceive as a dilemma between the moral stance of PD of sharing power and the fact that designers as experts in 'making' IT systems and artifacts have considerable power. Our ambition is to understand how participation in a design project is possible, given this dilemma: how much participation has to take place for a PD project to be participatory; how do participants know that they have participated? We base the book on two projects in which we have been involved as participatory designers. We use experiences from these books for exploring these questions.

Designing IT systems and artifacts involves a set of complex practices and there are many possible perspectives to take on this process. We start with decision-making in design, with a focus on those decisions that shape the design result. In doing this we look at the choices on which these decisions were based and at who participated in opening up these choices and who closed them in a decision. The focus on decision-making enables us to analyse the power relations that are 'at work' in a process that we describe as creating choices, selecting a choice, implementing and evaluating it. In a PD process these 'steps' are open to the contributions of all participants. Analysing the details and dynamics of decision-making helps us talk about participation in a more specific way.

1.1 About Participation in Design

Design is a generic term used for a whole range of practices that have some characteristics in common. Basically, design is about making things but as design historically appeared as different from craft, design is taken as the making of plans and specifications for things that others will build (e.g., architectural drawings, product or systems descriptions). This often separates the designers from their product and also from their prospective users. Suchman has discussed this as 'the view from nowhere' (Suchman 2002). There is ample evidence that specifications written in a language that is clear to professional readers are not easily understood by lay people like the average user. PD addresses this problem by enabling designers and users to communicate without this specific formal language, by for example using exemplars and prototypes as means for exploring the problem space and possible solutions during design (Bratteteig et al. 2010). In a PD project the running prototype tested 'in the wild' by users in a real use context may replace a specification document. Also, key to the practice of PD is that the analysis of an application area or problem space and the construction of the solution are inseparable (Schön 1983). Building a prototype is an intricate part of doing the analysis.

We also have to account for the fact that design deals with 'wicked problems': they are ill-defined and ill-structured, with the consequence that 'Problem understanding and problem resolution are concomitant to each other. [… The] process of solving the problem is identical with the process of understanding its nature' (Rittel and Webber 1973, p. 162). A result of this 'wickedness' is that most design processes are open-ended, often exploratory, and highly complex. Problem understanding ideally also involves questioning if a new technology is adequate and desirable and for whom.

Design work is also intensely collaborative, often requiring multidisciplinary expertise. In order to understand design we need to pay attention to

Design as a collaborative activity that sometimes involves a large network of actors (client, investor, specialists of all sorts, and more); the multidisciplinarity of design work, which influences the ways designers express, represent, and communicate an evolving design concept; the role of artefacts and materials; the diversity of material practices which shape the design object, their historical-cultural roots and specificity; and the multiplicity of the design object itself, its changing representations in different media, and how it gets translated/ transformed in the process of design. (Bratteteig et al. 2010, p. 39)

While having these common characteristics, design practices vary a lot according to what the artifact is that is being designed: is it a housing complex or an urban area, is it a teapot or a chair, is it a computer-based system or product? As concerns the design of computer-based systems and artifacts there is a large variety of things to be designed: particular, tailor-made systems for specific purposes and settings or generic products; new technologies or innovative applications of existing technologies; construction of user applications, application level applications or IT infrastructures. It is the envisioned design result that gives a particular design process its main characteristics as it drives the decisions about materials and resources. Not all forms of design imply users. However, participation in design is important at the point where the computer-based system or artifact meets the user, since this is where the experience, knowledge and creativity of users will make a difference for how the technology will be imagined and made concrete.

Drawing on (Schütz 1954, p. 106), we argue that design is an action 'upon the world', aimed at modifying parts of the world—particular artifacts—in order to better act 'within the world'. In PD, 'the world' refers to the users' practices, hence seeing the use context as the world that we act upon and the artifact's design as an embedded part of this context. The aim is not just to make the artifact itself, but also to address the way it enters into users' practices. The scope of the design process therefore also includes the future use context. The evaluation of the design result concerns the system or artifact itself, the way its machinery works and the artifact-in-use when it becomes part of a practice. While some artifacts have the potential of instigating changes of a practice, others may only change the ways users carry out particular activities.

This orientation towards future use means that PD needs to enrol both technical and use knowledge. Users are needed for arriving at adequate representations of 'how they do their work and indeed any other activities where they might use technology' (Robertson and Wagner 2012, p. 65), as well as in the co-creation of the artifact that may support their practice in a variety of ways. The technical knowledge is needed to imagine the ways in which a technology may contribute to supporting use and for conceptualizing and creating prototypal realizations of a system or artifact that can be evaluated and improved in use. The making of the artifact itself is hence only one element of the PD process.

As design problems are 'wicked' and 'ill-defined', an important part of the practice of design is to support the possibility to make choices that can be un-made if the trying out of a promising 'design move' did not have the wanted effect. The notion of 'design move' goes back to Schön and Wiggins who understood design as processes of 'seeing-moving-seeing': seeing and evaluating a situation, making a move to change the situation, and evaluating the result.

> A designer sees, moves and sees again. Working in some visual medium—drawing, in our examples—the designer sees what is 'there' in some representation of a site, draws in relation to it, and sees what has been drawn, thereby informing further designing. [...] The basic local unit of a design process, which we call a move experiment, involves several kinds of seeing, all dependent on visual apprehension, or literal seeing: the construction of figures or gestalts, which determine the things and relations in terms-of which the designer thinks; appreciation of the qualities in terms of which intentions are formed, problems are set, and solutions are judged; the recognition of intended and unintended consequences of moves. (Schön and Wiggins 1992, p. 135 and 154 f.)

Making a move means making a choice, hence closing off other choices (Stolterman 1991). However, the new situation that arises from the move also opens up new possibilities—new choices—that were not possible to foresee before the move was tried out. It goes without saying that this also concerns the design process at large: use practices that evolve around a new artifact are not possible to foresee before the artifact is there, even for experienced users. Important to add that as a collaborative practice, design work includes much more than the 'move experiments' Schön and Wiggins describe with a view onto the individual designer (Schön and Wiggins 1992): it requires planning a complex process of often distributed work with lots of interdependencies, negotiating the problem definition with multiple stakeholders, co-creating representations and design solutions, preparing for evaluation in use, and so forth.

Models of the design process often describe design as starting with an idea, proceeding to a vision, and approaching a solution (or a specification of a solution) through sketching. This kind of linear process is rarely followed in practice: rather the process 'jumps' between envisioning and activities like sketching, prototyping, and 'testing'. Architects have used the metaphor of 'meandering' to describe their work: 'Meandering means that the possibility to suspend a design decision or to re-open it even at a rather late stage of the planning process should be preserved' (Tellioglu et al. 1998). Bratteteig describes this in a slightly different way, as oscillating between levels of concretization and abstraction (Bratteteig et al. 2004; Löwgren and Stolterman 2007).

Hence, an important characteristic of design work is that it is open-ended. Lave talks about 'open-ended processes of improvisation with the social, material, and experiential resources at hand' (Lave and Wenger 1991, p. 13). The need to maintain openness in design has implications for how designers work. Openness means that decisions about possible design trajectories should not be made too quickly, and requires that the different actors present their contributions to the design in a form that is open to the possibility of change and in ways that enable choices to be unmade or changed as long as possible (Wagner 2004).

PD adds a strong normative dimension to design practice: to include practitioners or 'users' in the design process and have them participate in design decisions. That is, the practice of PD includes a reflective element: it requires participants to reflect on issues such as access, in/exclusion, voice, the dynamics of decision-making, etc. Moreover, there is a strong sense in the PD community that there are 'right ways' of practicing PD. There are different types of 'rules' at play in the practice of PD: rules that govern the organizing of the design process as such; rules that ensure participation; rules that support the collaborative imagining of a future design in use; and finally, rules that enable joint decision-making. We use the term 'rule' in the sense Wittgenstein used it: 'descriptively, to indicate *regularity* or as a criterion of *correct* conduct' (Schmidt 2011, p. 372).

In fact, the rich repertoire of methods, tools and techniques that participatory designers have developed over the last 20 and more years are intended to help practitioners to perform PD in 'the right way'. Some of these tools and techniques are to ensure that all participants have a chance to contribute and that their voices are heard. Others are to support the creative-experimental part of PD: the activities of 'telling, making and enacting' a future design (for an overview see, Brandt et al. 2012; Mörtberg et al. 2010).

In this book we seek to open up the idea that there is a right way of doing PD. But we also try to identify what distinguishes PD from other forms of user involvement.

1.2   About Power and Decision-Making in Design

As already stated, in PD designers are expected to involve future users in all stages of the decision-making process and to share power with them. This creates a rather particular situation within an organization or context. As we will show in our case analysis such a principled commitment does not make power issues disappear. Depending on the context of a project, the sharing of power may be made difficult by patterns of domination, based on hierarchical relationships and unequal access to resources within an organization; it may be hampered by the lack of respect for other knowledge traditions, based on cultural or gender differences. Power issues exist even in the presence of a strong commitment to giving all participants an equal voice.

Then the question is how to address these issues of power: on which aspects of this 'extremely troubling' concept (Pitkin 1973) to build our analysis. The distinction between 'power over' and 'power to' is a helpful starting point. 'Power over', getting another person to do something, very much depends on organizational resources: position (e.g. being the project leader), access to resources but also the capacity to resolve ambiguity, to set the agenda or to enrol. 'Power to' means agency: the capacity to shape action, which partly depends on access to organizational resources, partly on 'power/knowledge' in the Foucauldian sense: the power of defining issues, that means of 'normalizing' them so that they can be recognized and resolved; of translating them into a language that makes them amenable to particular interventions (at the expense of others).

Both, 'power over' and 'power to' are related to decision-making. This leads to the question what we mean when saying that a 'decision' has been taken. Much of the vast literature on decision-making in organizations still refers to Herbert Simon's notion of bounded rationality and decision-making as a three phase 'intelligence-design-choice' sequence (Simon 1960), which was taken up, refined, as well as contested by those who stressed 'anarchy' (as an extreme counterpart of rationality). The 'garbage can' model of Cohen et al. went perhaps farthest in describing organizational decision making as a chaotic process (Cohen et al. 1972). At the roots of this chaos may be ambiguity (of the aims, purposes or task descriptions), the need to account for many participants with divergent stakes, loose coupling between organizational units, and so forth. The literature also opens the very concept of 'decision' to further scrutiny.

From this debate we take several insights: the term 'decision' can be useful but also misleading. It 'may imply distinct, identifiable choice', although 'in fact many decisions cannot easily be pinned down, in time or in place' (Langley et al. 1995, p. 261). Often, we can only talk about a decision in retrospect or at least in moments of 'reflection-on-action', when we are able to identify choices and the decisions that have been taken given these choices. Also, and here we will refer to Schütz and his notion of the 'natural attitude' (Schütz 1954, p. 106), which characterizes most of our action in everyday life, decisions are intricately embedded in people's practices. Moreover, decisions are not isolated from each other but closely interrelated and linked. We are inspired by Langley et al. who propose to rather than looking for 'isolated traces of single decisions' conceive them 'in terms of continuing and interacting streams of issues that spin off actions, sometimes through identifiable decisions' (Langley et al. 1995, p. 270). We propose to look at decision-making in design as being accessible through examining the issues at stake and how they are interrelated.

We will also demonstrate that 'power' is only one way of looking at decision-making in PD. For example, as Pitkin argues, there is 'influence'. These concepts 'are not strictly comparable. They are of different kinds, or move in different dimensions' (Pitkin 1973, p. 279). So do other relevant concepts for understanding decision-making, such as 'trust' and 'loyalty'. As we will show a large number of 'decisions' in both design projects that we analyse in this book had been based on trust. More generally speaking, the sharing of power in PD is a complex interplay of mechanisms, in which different resources and multiple dependencies and loyalties come to work together.

1.3 The Cases

The discussion in this book is based on two cases. Both projects—*IPCity* and *Sisom*—were framed as PD projects and we participated in them as participatory designers. Why these two projects and why only two? Our argument here is that detailed knowledge of a project is necessary to be able to identify instances of decision-making (or better: interwoven networks of issues) and understand the role of power, influence, trust and loyalty in how these issues were resolved. This is not possible without a rather intimate knowledge of a project and the many details of a design process, including the things that participants do not want to talk about.

The handling of a complex network of issues in a project is rarely documented in ways that would easily allow the kind of analysis we present in this book. We had to 'dig deep' into the project archives, conduct interviews, and consult our memories as participants in the projects. Revisiting the projects together for this book brought forward aspects that we had not been aware of before.

The first case we have included in this book, *IPCity*, is the design of a collaborative mixed reality application, a project in which one of the authors has been central from its initiation to its end. The application aimed to support mixed teams of urban planners, politicians and citizens in using participatory technologies to create and manipulate design alternatives for real urban planning projects (Bratteteig et al. 2012; Maquil 2010; Maquil et al. 2007; Wagner 2011). The *MR-Tent* was evaluated and redesigned in six cycles of design–evaluation–redesign in the context of real (ongoing) urban planning projects with urban planners and a variety of interested participants as users. *Sisom*, the second case, is about an information system that allows patients to report their symptoms on a mobile device, before consulting a doctor. A previous system for adult patients had been a success, and the hospital wanted to develop a similar system for child patients. Children are, however, different from adults in several ways. For example, small children cannot read and write and do not understand abstract information well. A project was initiated, aimed at designing a children's version of the adult system for children with cancer (Ruland et al. 2008, 2009).

These two projects open up to questions of participation and power. Both have participatory results—they enlarge the action space for their users: offering new possibilities for citizen participation in urban projects; supporting very ill children in expressing and communicating their symptoms. However, none of the projects was participatory in a 'straightforward' way. First of all, there were different types of users in both projects. *IPCity* aimed at including common citizens but primarily collaborated with urban planning experts; *Sisom* targeted children with cancer but used healthy children as substitutes and cooperated mainly with health care professionals. *IPCity* was a research project with a strong experimental character but within the 'real' context of urban projects. It implemented a participatory approach to urban planning on the basis of architectural concepts, trying to nurture novel practices. Its result, the *Mixed Reality Tent*, was not so much useful in a practical sense than generating knowledge about how to represent urban situations so that non-experts, in collaboration with experts, could produce and debate visions of the future of a site. *Sisom* was a development project, aiming at a product and service, which would fit traditional practices in the hospital. The core of the project was framed as 'translating' medical terms into how children would talk about their symptoms and representing them in an easily understandable and motivating way. The outcome of this project was useful in a practical way.

We think that the fact that these two projects represent different practice fields, approaches to design, and orientations (research versus product development) enabled us to identify issues that are of potential relevance for a more general analysis of power and decision-making in PD.

1.4 Overview of the book

A complex topic is always difficult to approach analytically, since multiple interdependencies are difficult to grasp and explicate in a linear-sequential way. For example, it is difficult to write about decision-making without referring to issues of power.

We decided to start with decision-making. This is based on our conviction that talking about power in PD in the concrete way we aspire to presupposes a rather detailed analysis of decision-making in a project. Hence, the book starts with a chapter that explores the notion of decision-making or making choices. We then introduce the case material and describe the choices that were opened up in both projects and who participated in creating these choices and selecting among them. This part is mostly descriptive, following a set of distinctions we found useful: between big decisions concerning the vision of the project; decisions on how to implement the vision; decision requiring negotiations with the outside world; and nondecisions. An important next step in this analysis is identifying linkages between these different decisions. Decisions in complex contexts are rarely 'stand-alone'. They affect the space for action, excluding some choices while opening up for others. The fact that some decisions carry more weight then others is important for understanding how power is exercised in a PD project; so is the dynamics of creating choices and selecting.

Understanding decision-making has prepared the grounds for discussing issues of power and participation. We start by introducing views onto power that seem useful for our analysis, to then look more deeply into three aspects of power: how decisions in the two projects were shaped by structural arrangements; which 'mechanisms' participants used to align their work and different positions, finding instances of 'power to' but also of influence, trust and loyalty in how choices were introduced and selected. We also discuss issues of power/knowledge, examining in particular how topics were constructed through 'discourse' and exploring instances of 'normalising practices'.

Participation is the final topic we address and the way we discuss it is shaped by our preceding analysis of decision-making and power. In this chapter we ask: who was involved, which decisions were made in a participatory way and which were not. This is an attempt at grasping the depth of participation. We argue that even though there may be limitations to sharing power in a PD project, it may have a participatory design result. Furthermore, a participatory result would not have been possible without any user participation in creating choices, even though critical decisions may have been taken in a non-participatory way.

The concluding chapter looks back at how decisions were made, how power was enacted and at participation, emphasizing the importance of a participatory vision.

References

Andersen, N. E., Kensing, F., Lundin, J., Mathiassen, L., Munk-Madsen, A., Rasbech, M., & Sørgaard, P. (1990). *Professional systems development: Experience, ideas and action.* Upper Saddle River: Prentice-Hall.

Beck, E. (2002). P for political: Participation is not enough. *Scandinavian Journal of Information Systems, 14*(1), 77–92.

Bermann, T. (1985). Not only windmills: female service workers and new technologies. *Proceedings of the IFIP WG 9.1 first working conference on woman, work and computerization: Opportunities and disadvantages* (North-Holland: Amsterdam). pp. 231–248.

Bermann, T., & Thoresen, K. (1988). Can networks make an organization? *Proceedings of the 1988 ACM conference on computer-supported cooperative work, Association for Computing Machinery,* pp. 153–166.

Bjerknes, G., & Bratteteig, T. (1995). User participation and democracy. A discussion of Scandinavian research on systems development. *Scandinavian Journal of Information Systems, 7*(1), 73–98.

Bjerknes, G., Ehn, P., & Kyng, M. (Eds.). (1987). *Computers and democracy—A scandinavian challenge.* Avebury: Aldershot.

Bjørn-Andersen, N., & Hedberg, B. (1977). Designing information systems in an organizational perspective. *Studies in the Management Sciences, 5,* 125–142. (Prescriptive models of organizations).

Blomberg, J., Giacomi, J., Mosher, A., & Swenton-Wall, P. (1993). Ethnographic field methods and the relation to design. In D. Schuler & A. Namioka (Eds.), *Participatory design: Principles and practices* (pp. 123–156). Hillsdale: Lawrence Erlbaum.

Bødker, K., Kensing, F., & Simonsen, J. (2004). *Participatory IT design: Designing for business and workplace realities.* Cambridge: The MIT Press.

Brandt, E., Binder, T., & Sanders, E. (2012). Tools and techniques: Ways to engage telling, making and enacting. In J. Simonsen & T. Robertson (Eds.), *Routledge international handbook of participatory design* (pp. 145–181). London: Routledge.

Bratteteig, T. (2004). *Making change. Dealing with relations between design and use.* Dr. Philos dissertation, University of Oslo, Oslo.

Bratteteig, T., & Wagner, I. (2012). Spaces for participatory creativity. *CoDesign, 8*(2-3), 105–126.

Bratteteig, T., Wagner, I., Morrison, A., Stuedahl, D., & Mörtberg, C. (2010). Research practices in digital design. In I. Wagner, T. Bratteteig, & D. Stuedahl (Eds.), *Exploring digital design* (pp. 17–54). London: Springer.

Bratteteig, T., Bødker, K., Dittrich, Y., Mogensen, P. H., & Simonsen, J. (2012). Methods: Organising principles and general guidelines for participatory design projects. In J. Simonsen & T. Robertson (Eds.), *Routledge international handbook of participatory design* (pp. 177–144). London: Routledge.

Briefs, U., Claudio, U., & Schneider, L. (Eds.). (1983). *Systems design for, with, and by the users.* Amsterdam: North Holland.

Clement, A., & Van den Besselaar, P. (1993). A retrospective look at PD projects. *Communications of the ACM, 36*(6), 29–37.

Cohen, M. D., March, J. G., & Olsen, J. P. (1972). A garbage can model of organizational choice. *Administrative Science Quarterly, 17*(1), 1–25.

Doherty, P., Fuchs-Kittowski, K., Kolm, P., & Mathiassen, L. (Eds.). (1987). *System design for human development and productivity: Participation and beyond.* Amsterdam: North-Holland.

Ehn, P. (1989). *Work-oriented design of computer artifacts.* Hillsdale: Lawrence Erlbaum.

Ehn, P., & Sandberg, Å. (1979). *Företagsstyrning och löntagarmakt: Planering, datorer, organisation och fackligt utredningsarbete.* Stockholm: Prisma/Arbetslivscentrum.

Floyd, C., Mehl, W. M., Reisin, F. M., Schmidt, G., & Wolf, G. (1989). Out of Scandinavia: Alternative approaches to software design and system development. *Human-Computer Interaction, 4*(4), 253–350.

Gärtner, J., & Wagner, I. (1996). Mapping actors and agenda: Political frameworks of design & participation. *Human-Computer Interaction,11,* 187–214.

Greenbaum, J. (1993). A design of one's own: Towards participatory design in the United States. In D. Schuler & A. Namioka (Eds.), *Participatory design: Principles and practices* (pp. 27–37). New York: Lawrence Erlbaum.

Greenbaum, J., & Kyng, M. (Eds.). (1991). *Design at work: Cooperative design of computer work.* Hillsdale: Lawrence Erlbaum.

Hughes, J. A., Randall, D., & Shapiro, D. (1992). From ethnographic record to system design. *Computer Supported Cooperative Work (CSCW), 1*(3), 123–141.

Kensing, F. (2003). *Methods and practices in participatory design.* Copenhagen: ITU Press.

Kyng, M. (2010). On the next practices of participatory design. *Scandinavian Journal of Information Systems, 22*(1), 49–68.

Langley, A., Mintzberg, H., Pitcher, P., Posada, E., & Saint-Macary, J. (1995). Opening up decision-making. *Organization Science, 6*(3), 260–279.

Lave, J., & Wenger, E. (1991). *Situated learning: Legitimate peripheral participation.* Cambridge: Cambridge University Press.

Löwgren, J., & Stolterman, E. (2007). *Thoughtful interaction design: A design perspective on information technology. Cambridge*: MIT Press.

Mambrey, P., Mark, G., & Pankoke-Babatz, U. (1998). User advocacy in participatory design: Designers' experiences with a new communication channel. *Computer Supported Cooperative Work (CSCW), 7*(3/4), 291–313.

Maquil, V. (2010). *The ColorTable: An interdisciplinary design process.* Wien: Vienna University of Technology.

Maquil, V., Psik, T., Wagner, I., & Wagner, M. (4–7 Nov 2007). *Expressive interactions supporting collaboration in urban design.* Paper presented at the proceedings of GROUP 2007, Sanibel Island, Florida, USA.

Mathiassen, L. (1997). *Computers and design in context.* Cambridge: The MIT Press.

Mörtberg, C., Bratteteig, T., Wagner, I., Stuedahl, D., & Morrison, A. (2010). Methods that matter in digital design research. In I. Wagner, T. Bratteteig, & D. Stuedahl (Eds.), *Exploring digital design* (pp. 105–144). London: Springer.

Muller, M. (1993). Pictive: Democratizing the dynamics of the design session. In D. Schuler & A. Namioka (Eds.), *Participatory design: Principles and practices* (pp. 211–237). New York: Lawrence Erlbaum.

Nygaard, K. (1979). The iron and metal project: Trade union participation. *Computers Dividing Man and Work, 13,* 94–107.

Nygaard, K., & Sørgård, P. (1987). The perspective concept in informatics. In G. Bjerknes, P. Ehn, & M. Kyng (Eds.), *Computers and democracy-a Scandinavian challenge* (pp. 371–393). Avebury: Gower Publishing.

Pape, T. C., & Thoresen, K. (1992). Evolutionary prototyping in a change perspective: A tale of three municipalities. *Information Technology & People, 6*(2/3), 145–170.

Pitkin, H. F. (1973). *Wittgenstein and justice.* Berkeley: University of California Press.

Rittel, H. W., & Webber, M. M. (1973). Dilemmas in a general theory of planning. *Policy Sciences, 4*(2), 155–169.

Robertson, T. (1998). Shoppers and tailors: Participative practices in small Australian design companies. *Computer Supported Cooperative Work, 7,* 205–221.

Robertson, T. (2006). Ethical issues in interaction design. *Ethics and Information Technology, 8*(2), 49–59.

Robertson, T., & Wagner, I. (2012). Ethics: Engagement, representation and politics-in-action. In J. Simonsen & T. Robertson (Eds.), *Routledge international handbook of participatory design* (pp. 64–85). London: Routledge.

Ruland, C. M., Starren, J., & Vatne, T. M. (2008). Participatory design with children in the development of a support system for patient-centered care in pediatric oncology. *Journal of Biomedical Informatics, 41*(4), 624–635.

Ruland, C. M., Hamilton, G. A., & Schjødt-Osmo, B. (2009). The complexity of symptoms and problems experienced in children with cancer: A review of the literature. *Journal of Pain and Symptom Management, 37*(3), 403–418.

Schmidt, K. (2011). *Cooperative work and coordinative practices.* New York: Springer.

Schön, D. A. (1983). *The reflective practitioner.* Harper Collins. New York: Basic Books.

Schön, D. A., & Wiggins, G. (1992). Kinds of seeing and their function in designing. *Design Studies, 13,* 135–156.

Schuler, D., & Namioka, A. (Eds.). (1993). *Participatory design: Principles and practices.* New York: Lawrence Erlbaum.

Schütz, A. (1954). Concept and theory formation in the social sciences. *The Journal of Philosophy,* 51(9), 257–273.

Shapiro, D. (2010). A modernised participatory design? A response to Kyng. *Scandinavian Journal of Information Systems, 22*(1), 69–76.

Simon, H. (1960). *The new science of managerial decision.* New York: Harper and Row.

Simonsen, J., & Robertson, T. (2012). *International handbook of participatory design.* London: Routledge.

Stolterman, E. (1991). Designarbetets dolda rationalitet: en studie av metodik och praktik inom systemutveckling. PhD thesis, University of Umeå, Umeå.

Suchman, L. (1995). Making work visible. *Communications of the Association for Computing Machinery, 38*(9), 56 ff.

Suchman, L. (2002). Located accountabilities in technology production. *Scandinavian Journal of Information Systems, 14*(2), 91–106.

Tellioglu, H., Wagner, I., & Lainer, R. (1998). *Open design methodologies. Exploring architectural practice for systems design.* Paper presented at the *proceedings of PDC'98,* Seattle.

Thorsrud, E., Sorensen, B. A., & Gustavsen, B. (1976). Sociotechnical approach to industrial democracy in Norway. In R. Dubin (Ed.), *Handbook of work organization and society* (pp. 648–687). Chicago: Rand McNally.

Wagner, I. (1993). A web of fuzzy problems: Confronting the ethical issues in systems design. *Communications of the Association for Computing Machinery,*36(6), 94–101 (Special issue on participative design).

Wagner, I. (2004). Open planning—A reflection on methods. In R. Boland & F. Collopy (Eds.), *Managing as designing* (pp. 153–163). Stanford: Stanford University Press.

Wagner, I. (2011). Building urban narratives: Collaborative site-seeing and envisioning in the MR tent. *Computer Supported Cooperative Work (CSCW), 21*(1), 1–42.

Wynn, E. (1991). Taking practice seriously. In J. Greenbaum & M. Kyng (Eds.), *Design at work: Cooperative design of computer systems* (pp. 45–64). Hillsdale: Lawrence Erlbaum.

Chapter 2
Decision-Making in Design

Design is a process of generating choices and choosing among them; taking decisions is a fundamental element of design. Both concepts, decision and choice, are used almost interchangeably in economic as well as in organization theory. They are, however, slightly different. While a decision is 'a conclusion or resolution reached after consideration' and decision-making 'the action or process of deciding something or of resolving a question', a choice is 'an act of selecting or making a decision when faced with two or more possibilities': 'it presupposes a range of possibilities from which one or more may be chosen' (Oxford Dictionary). We prefer to talk about choices, as in design there are always alternatives to choose from; and when talking about the process we use the notion of decision-making.

PD suggests making design decisions in a participative way, but in order to understand in what and how users participate we need to have a better picture about the decision-making in question. In this chapter we aim to arrive at a more precise and operational concept of decision-making (in design). We start out with theories that explain and explore decision-making, to continue in the next chapters to apply some of the concepts to our two cases.

2.1 About Decision Making

Decision-making is a topic that has been addressed primarily by organizational sociologists. As mentioned before, much of the debate still refers to Herbert Simon's notions of bounded rationality and decision-making as a three phase 'intelligence-design-choice' sequence (Simon 1960). The model has been much discussed and contested, in particular by those who emphasized bounded rationality—or seemingly irrational behavior in organizations (Feldman and March 1981). An alternative model is the 'garbage can' model (Cohen et al. 1972) that went far in describing organizational decision making as a chaotic process. The garbage can metaphor had been inspired by the notion of 'muddling through', which Lindblom in his analysis of policy-making described as being 'both praised as a highly sophisticated form of problem-solving and denounced as no method at all', adding 'because it will be su-

T. Bratteteig, I. Wagner, *Disentangling Participation*, Computer Supported
Cooperative Work, DOI 10.1007/978-3-319-06163-4_2,
© Springer International Publishing Switzerland 2014

perior to any other decision-making method available for complex problems in many circumstances, certainly superior to a futile attempt at superhuman comprehensiveness' (Lindblom 1959, p. 188). In line with this view is Rittel and Webber's concern that 'planning problems are inherently wicked' (Rittel and Webber 1973, p. 160), contrasting real world problems with 'tame' problems in systems like mathematics and chess. 'Wicked problems' are inherently indefinite, difficult to describe and solve.

Decision-making is indeed a complex topic, also when the decisions are design decisions. Here we have to bear in mind that design as a practice of making is different from most of the practices the organizational literature refers to, including policy-planning. However, the mentioned models and concepts fit well with Schön's view that the definition or setting of a problem is deeply intertwined with its solution: a problem is often not fully understood or described before a solution has been reached (Schön 1983). Schön described design practice as 'move experiments', which involve different kinds of seeing: seeing 'what is there' (what has been drawn, built) as well as seeing and judging ('is this how it should be', 'does it work'?), before taking the next move (Schön 1995). 'Seeing-moving-seeing' is a process, in which problems are set and solutions are found and evaluated. Even if Schön and Wiggins look at the first stages of a design project, using an architect performing initial sketches as an example, they address the important insight that what we might call a 'decision' is an integral part of design practice. This has also been stressed by Alby and Zucchermaglio, who observed engineers repairing an IT system, yet another example of design work. They remark:

> Contrary to traditional problem-solving models (in which the analysis phase precedes and is completely separated from the successive intervention), here the problem is actually analysed by making an incremental series of small interventions. (Alby and Zucchermaglio 2006, p. 961)

Typical of design is a process of decision-making which proceeds through doing and judging the results of this doing, which become visible in an artifact, be it a prototype of something novel or a system that is supposed to run smoothly. We should remember, however, that a PD project is intensely collaborative—as are most design projects -, with people convening to discuss, propose, evaluate solutions (in use), and so forth. These are activities where the 'seeing' of the solitary designer that Schön observed is complemented by argumentation and reflection, and more explicit types of 'decisions' will be taken. Moreover, in PD much effort is spent on understanding the (work) practices of future users. This involves activities, such as observing the practice and developing shared representations of it, on which the design can build. The fact that a use practice can never be fully represented except through users themselves participating adds a range of new criteria to the making and evaluating of design choices. Similarly, 'testing' an evolving prototype in use involves observation, the joint critical assessment of these observations and, eventually, new 'move experiments'. Finally, all design practices—design of IT systems or buildings—involve mundane activities, such as making calculations, scheduling, compiling information from producers (of building elements), handing plans over to others for them to control, complete, annotate, and so forth. All these activities involve choices.

2.2 Making Choices

We think it is helpful here to recur to the work of Alfred Schütz who has developed a theory of everyday action together with a theory of signs and symbols, in which the human capacity to transcend the immediate experience plays a key role. He initially assumed a phenomenologist position, with the aim to provide a sound epistemological basis for Max Weber's notion of 'meaningful action', which he sought in the philosophy of Henri Bergson and the phenomenology of Edmund Husserl (Hitzler 1987). Later he also developed an interest in philosophical-anthropological questions, seeking an understanding of 'human experience' in its different forms (Knoblauch 1992).

Schütz was foremost interested in what he called the 'natural attitude', which is typical of daily life. Here we are 'geared into the world', which 'is the scene and also the object of our actions and interactions' (Schütz 1954, p. 106, 534). It is a world given to us. When acting in this world, we can rely on a certain 'stock of knowledge' ('Wissensvorrat'), which results from the sedimentation of previous experience. In daily life much of our action is habitualized: it is characterized by a 'suspension of doubt'. Hence, much of our choices or decision-making in daily life is embedded in the ways we frame a situation, on 'my knowledge of previously performed acts which are similar to the prescribed one, upon my knowledge of typically relevant features of the situation in which this projected action will occur, including my personal biographically determined situation' (Schütz 1962, p. 69).

So, the question is, how can we understand situations beyond everyday life, when we, for example, engage in a design project? In 'Choosing among projects of action' Schütz describes situations that involve choices between alternative 'projects' (Schütz 1962). He quotes John Dewey who wrote about such a choice as being preceded by 'a dramatic rehearsal in imagination of various competing possible lines of action. It is an experiment in making various combinations of selected elements of habits and impulses to see what the resultant action would be like if it were entered upon' (Dewey 1922, p. 190). For Schütz such moments of 'dramatic rehearsal' apply to situations in which our knowledge of possibilities becomes problematic, questionable, or open. In these moments we have to suspend belief in what we take for granted. This is to say that choice only happens in situations which 'give rise to a decisive new experience: the experience of doubt, of questioning, of choosing and deciding, in short, of deliberation' (Schütz 1951, p. 169):

> All projecting consists in an anticipation of future conduct by way of phantasying. ... Metaphorically speaking I have to have some idea of the structure to be erected before I can draft the blueprints. In order to project my future action as it will roll on I have to place myself in my phantasy at a future time when this action will already have been accomplished, when the resulting act will already have been materialized. Only then may I reconstruct the single steps which will have brought forth this future act. (Schütz 1951, p. 162)

There has been a debate if Schütz would endorse the rational choice model (e.g., Esser 1993). He himself has been rather clear about this. In 'The problem of rationality in the social world' he refers to the different meanings connected with the term 'rationality': reasonable, deliberate, planned or projected, predictable, logical, implicating 'a choice between two or more means toward the same end, or even between two different ends, and a selection of the most appropriate' (Schütz 1943, p. 104, 138 ff.); to conclude: '… the ideal of rationality is not and cannot be a peculiar feature of every-day thought, nor can it, therefore, be a methodological principle of the interpretation of human acts in daily life' (ibid, p. 142). It is, however, a characteristic of the (social) sciences that have developed their specific 'systems of rational action'. This does not mean that we cannot find examples of rational choice in everyday action. However, in daily life action is based on levels of clearness and explicitness that the actor's practical interests require. The rationality of our choices has to be seen in relation to the practical purposes we pursue. This is an important observation: it subordinates an abstract ideal of rationality to the purposes and the necessities at hand.

Schütz stresses the 'pragmatic motive' as well as the purposefulness of everyday action, and that our everyday actions aim at 'modifying' and 'dominating' the world by making changes to it: acting purposefully upon the world is fundamental to human action.

> The world of everyday life is the scene and also the object of our actions and interactions. We have to dominate it and we have to change it in order to realize the purposes which we pursue within it among our fellow-men. Thus, we work and operate not only within but upon the world. Our bodily movements—kinaesthetic, locomotive, operative—gear, so to speak, into the world, modifying or changing its objects and their mutual relationships. On the other hand, these objects offer resistance to our acts which we have either to overcome or to which we have to yield. In this sense it may be correctly said that a pragmatic motive governs our natural attitude toward the world of daily life. World, in this sense, is something that we have to modify by our actions or that modifies our actions. (Schütz 1945, p. 105, 534)

Designing is a particular way of modifying the world, of working 'upon it'. Schütz contends that 'the more the mind turns away from life, the larger the slabs of the everyday world of working which are put in doubt' (ibid, p. 554). The mind turning away from life is the mind that looks into a variety of different futures. PD is about envisioning the future and about turning this vision into something that can be used in the future. Imagining is central to this capacity: it is through imagining that we generate choices that can be examined, made material, and evaluated.

2.3   The Role of Imagination

Much work about imagination refers to Kant and his writings on 'aesthetic reflective judgment'. Even if Kant never defined imagination thoroughly, different forms can be distinguished in his work. One form of imagination is what he calls the productive imagination of cognition. It is 'the very ground of our having a world of experience at all': it 'arranges and presents the material of the "selective" manifold of re-production in such a way that Understanding can complete the cognitive synthesis' (Hume 1970, p. 487). So, imagination is a prerequisite for grasping the world intellectually. It mediates between what we capture with our senses and the categories for expressing our experience; it is a source of flexibility in cognition.

Kant also refers to another form: the free play of imagination, which is a more creative form, seemingly 'out on a short leash', as Hume states:

> It is important to note that imaginative representations are non-conceptual; the imaginative "idea" is a "transcendent" one for which no corresponding cognitive experience can be shown to exist. Therefore aesthetic "ideas" are "in-exponible"; they cannot be reduced to concepts, and so they cannot be subjected to cognitive extension. (Hume 1970, p. 488)

We are able to imagine without being bound by the constraints of cognition and morality, says Kant. We can imagine freely, playing with forms and meanings; or materialize our imaginings or 'aesthetic ideas' in a piece of art. Central to this imaginative free play is that it cannot be 'grasped discursively'—Kant treats it as a 'faculty of illusion'.

There is, however, a third meaning of imagination in Kant's work where it is treated as a powerful creative faculty:

> For the imagination (as a productive cognitive power) is very mighty when it creates, as it were, another nature out of the material that actual nature gives it.... In this process we feel our freedom from the law of association... for although it is under that law that nature lends us material, yet we can process that material into something quite different, namely, into something that surpasses nature. (Kant, The Critique of Judgment, 314, sec. 49; quoted after Kneller (1990))

It is this creative power, together with imaginative freedom, which allows us construct better futures. Imagination in these different readings complements 'sensibility' and 'intellect' in producing novel ideas and concepts.

Is this what Schütz means by 'phantasying'—having 'to place myself in my phantasy at a future time when this action will already have been accomplished, when the resulting act will already have been materialized' (Schütz 1951, p. 162)? We think that Schütz adds an important aspect by coupling 'phantasying' with 'projecting', seeing them as motivated by purpose and the 'practicability of the project' (Schütz 1951, p. 165). Imagination requires transgressing the boundaries of the known and of conventions of seeing things. We need to go beyond what we normally take for granted, what Schütz calls 'suspend' our beliefs in how everyday activities happen. However, designing requires moving beyond the free play of imagination giving it a purposeful direction.

Schütz' arguments help understand the practice of PD, where 'imaginative freedom' is bound by the commitment to support better ways of performing a practice in the future; and not only so. What we are able to imagine is bound by our cultural-historically inherited collective imaginaries; by the discourses that define and produce the objects of our knowledge and influence how ideas are put into practice; and by (in)vested interests, time, already-existing conditions, and so forth, all of which are part of the 'politics' of PD—a point we will elaborate in our analysis of power issues (see Chap. 6).

Creativity then seems to what is needed to move from imagination to something tangible—in the case of PD: a design. Creativity is about moving from 'imaginative' possibilities to a choice:

A creative event occurs as the moment of insight at which a problem-solution pair is framed: what Schön called 'problem framing'. Studies of expert and outstanding designers suggest that this framing ability is crucial to high-level performance in creative design. (Dorst and Cross 2001, p. 435)

The role of imagination in design work has been widely discussed, however not so much in a conceptual way (Folkmann 2010 being an exception). Schön's empirical studies demonstrate the linkages between problem setting and problem solving, making design a process of 'naming and framing', widening the idea space by 'seeing-as' and 'what-if' (Lanzara 1983). Design processes include working on three interacting levels of abstraction: the abstract vision, the concrete operative image, and the formalized design specification (Bratteteig and Stolterman 1997; Löwgren and Stolterman 2007). The vision guides the design in making choices, and 'provides a tension between what is and what should be and, … it also provides the direction in which the restructuring presses forward' (Arnheim 1962, p. 8). These general concepts characterize design practices rather than help us analyze the role of imagination in design.

How can we understand the 'imagining' part in PD? In PD a variety of techniques are used to support imagining. They help designers and users explore, think, tell and enact differently by emphasizing the value of sharing and understanding each other's imaginings (Bratteteig et al. 2012). Hence, PD builds on 'imaginative acts' that are made concrete in the form of e.g. stories, visual material or playful enactments.

How can moving from 'imaginative acts' to choices be understood? John Dewey, in writing of creative power, stresses: 'Not even a useful object is produced except by the intervention of imagination' (Dewey 2005/1934, p. 285). He then describes the interplay of imagination and working with concrete material, which is central to design:

Whether a musician, painter or architect works out his original emotional idea in terms of auditory or visual imaginary or in the actual medium as he works is of relative minor importance. For the imagery is of the objective medium undergoing development. The physical media may be ordered in imagination or in concrete material. In any case, the physical process develops imagination, while imagination is conceived in terms of concrete material. Only by the progressive organization of "inner" and "outer" material in organic connection with each other can anything be produced that is not a learned document or an illustration of something familiar. (Dewey 2005/1934, p. 78)

Dewey stresses the importance of concrete material for the process of imagining when it comes to creating something that can be built or painted or written. This resonates with the practice of the Russian designer Vladimir Tatlin who held that design should 'derive from exploring and exploiting a material's intrinsic qualities, and be considering how it might combine with other materials' (quoted in Fredrickson 1999, p. 53). Imagination, says Dewey, creates choices when it brings the 'inner' and 'outer' material together. The view that the material guides the design is common in literature on design and craft (Harper 1987; Ingold 2013; Jung and Stolterman 2012; Pye 1964). Design knowledge is embodied and action-based (Bratteteig 2004; Molander 1996).

We think it important to move away from 'mentalist' interpretations of creativity in design. Creativity depends on contextual as well as individual elements (Amabile 1996; Kaufmann 2006, p. 212); it is based on individual competencies (Kaufman 2004,

p. 211). In problem solving that requires competence, creativity has to do with the ability to reformulate the problem so as to create a broader problem space (Csikszentmihalyi 1997; Metcalfe and Wiebe 1987). This is an argument for including the perspectives of users in the process of 'naming and framing' (Schön 1983) so that the number of choices—and the scope of problems and solutions—is broadened beyond the designers' initial imagination (Bratteteig 2004; Bratteteig and Stolterman 1997). While this could be read as a purely 'instrumental' use of users in design, PD takes a normative stance, claiming the right of users to participate in decisions that affect their lives.

Schön strengthens a notion of imagining that is grounded in the concrete practice of design. We could say that while engaging in 'move experiments'—sketching, interacting with materials—designers make use of imagination and it is this imagining that widens their choices. With each design move some of these choices are closed, while evaluation of the move and reflection open up for new choices. Not only that: when Schön refers to 'reflection-in-action' he speaks of acting in a mindful way:

> And we also have the ability to reflect-in-action to generate new knowing, as when a jazz band improvises within a framework of meter, melody, and harmony: the pianist laying down "Sweet Sue" in a particular way, and the clarinetist listening to it and picking it up differently because of what the pianist is doing-and nobody using words. (Schön 1995, p. 30)

The jazz band is an interesting example, since it refers to a collaborative activity. Whilst performing, the musicians pick up what the others are playing, integrating it and jointly producing 'new knowing'. Here imagination becomes part of reflection-in-action: 'The actor reflects "in action" in the sense that his thinking occurs in an action-present—a stretch of time within which it is still possible to make a difference to the outcomes of action' (ibid).

Crucial for the purpose of our argument is the salience of imagination to the human condition, its disruptive potential, as well as its potential to—in combination with a reflective, mindful attitude and a 'purpose'—open up new choices.

2.4 Decision-Making in PD

So far we have established a link between human action, imagination, reflection, and choice. Next we have to argue why this link is fundamental to understanding the practice of PD. It is again Dewey, who has had much influence on how we understand design today, who has provided a beautiful description of how we make choices, again referring to 'imagination'. He says that in deliberation

> each conflicting habit and impulse takes its turn in projecting itself upon the screen of imagination. It unrolls a picture of its future history, of the career it would have if it were given head. ... In thought as well as in overt action, the objects experienced in following out a course of action attract, repel, satisfy, annoy, promote and retard. Thus deliberation proceeds. To say at last that it ceases is to say that choice, decision, takes place. What then is choice? Simply hitting in imagination upon an object which furnishes an adequate stimulus to the recovery of overt action ... Choice is not the emergence of preference out of indifference. It is the emergence of a unified preference out of competing preferences. (Dewey 1922, p. 134)

In deliberation we let each choice 'project itself upon the screen of imagination', we are weighing their possible consequences for the future. The choice we finally make is not a result of 'indifference'—but of what? Dewey talks about competing preferences: where do these come from?

The practice of PD is collaborative and interdisciplinary; it involves different 'stakeholders', each of which may have their own specific perspective and approach. A lot has been written about the role of ethnography in PD as fostering the co-creation of representations of a field of practice in which practitioners can recognize themselves and what they are engaged in doing (Blomberg and Karasti 2013). Some of the choices in PD emerge from these ethnographic accounts and the ways the different participants 'read' them. Other choices open up while participants engage in imagining possible futures. PD projects use techniques that help participants widen their choices rather than close down the problem/solution space too early, to handle openness and multiplicity:

> Openness implies that decisions about possible design trajectories are not made too quickly, and requires that the different actors present their work in a form that is open to the possibility of change. It puts emphasis on the dynamics of opening and expanding, fixing and constraining, re-opening, etc. (Tellioglu et al. 1998)

In PD, as in design work in general, this enlarging of the design space and maintaining it open to the possibility of change is critical. This can be stimulated by the presence of inspirational resources, which provide an element of surprise and discovery and help participants see things differently. Such inspirational resources are ubiquitous: they range from objects of daily life to pictures, movies, poetry, and metaphorical text. Moreover, designers and users create a range of design artifacts that help them concretize their imagining, making particular choices open to scrutiny and reflection.

> Engaging with a plethora of materials—inspirational resources as well as material conceptualizations of the design concept (text, diagrams, comics, video, sketches, rough "sketch" models, virtual 3D models, CAD drawings), with the diversity of design artifacts increasing the designer's possibilities of evaluating the design, as each representation helps make particular aspects of a design visible. (Binder et al. 2011, p. 21)

Again other choices open up when designers are engaged in making 'move experiments', imagining and 'reflecting-in-action'. A particularity of designing IT artifacts, to which we will come back in our analysis, is that choices are made material in an evolving set of prototypal realizations of a design concept or idea that can be 'tested' in more or less real situations of use. Finally, PD as a practice also involves making the joint decision-making practice possible, again by introducing specific methods and techniques that encourage postponing decisions on a problem/solution as long as possible by making the PD project a safe ground for alternative ways of seeing things: by, for example, pointing out hitherto 'invisible' details of a practice; being skeptical of ready-at-hand solutions or of claims that some things be 'unchangeable'; and so forth. It requires, to use Schütz, a suspension of the 'natural attitude' for participants to be able to step back in a process of reflection, deliberation, and choice.

Going back to the theme of organizational decision-making, we have to ask ourselves how the ideal that different voices are to be heard, understood and heeded for in a process can withstand further scrutiny. When PD makes different stakeholders meet and collaborate, just the multiplicity of perspectives, values and knowledges will make it difficult for all participants to attain 'levels of clearness and explicitness' about all the issues at stake in a project. We will therefore take a closer look at our two cases of PD projects.

2.5 Summary

Decision-making is a complex matter, even more so in design, where every design move involves choices. In this chapter we have aimed at becoming more precise about how design is decision-making and what role design decisions play in design and in PD. In design—as in everyday life—we make choices and select among them. In design, this takes the form of making moves, seeing some of the effects of the moves, and acting accordingly by moving back or making a new move.

References

Alby, F., & Zucchermaglio, C. (2006). How situated work practices shape group decision making. *Organization Studies, 27*(7), 943–966.

Amabile, T. M. (1996). *Creativity in context: Update to "the social psychology of creativity"*. Boulder: Westview Press.

Arnheim, R. (1962). *The genesis of a painting, Picasso's Guernica*. Berkley: University of California Press.

Binder, T., Ehn, P., Jacucci, G., De Michelis, G., Linde, P., & Wagner, I. (2011). *Design things*. Cambridge: MIT Press.

Blomberg, J., & Karasti, H. (2013). Reflections on 25 years of ethnography in CSCW. *Computer Supported Cooperative Work (CSCW), 22*(4–6) 1–51.

Bratteteig, T. (2004). *Making change. Dealing with relations between design and use*. Dr. Philos dissertation, University of Oslo, Oslo.

Bratteteig, T., & Stolterman, E. (1997). Design in groups—and all that jazz. In M. Kyng & L. Mathiasen (Eds.), *Computers and design in context* (pp. 289–316). Cambridge: MIT Press.

Bratteteig, T., Bødker, K., Dittrich, Y., Mogensen, P. H., & Simonsen, J. (2012). Methods: Organising principles and general guidelines for participatory design projects. In J. Simonsen & T. Robertson (Eds.), *Routledge international handbook of participatory design* (pp. 177–144). London: Routledge.

Cohen, M. D., March, J. G., & Olsen, J. P. (1972). A garbage can model of organizational choice. *Administrative Science Quarterly, 17*(1), 1–25.

Csikszentmihalyi, M. (1997). *Creativity. Flow and the psychology of discovery and invention*. New York: Harper.

Dewey, J. (1922). *Human nature and conduct: An introduction to social psychology*. New York: Carlton House.

Dewey, J. (2005/1934). *Art as experience*. Perigree Trade. New York: Perigee Books.

Dorst, K., & Cross, N. (2001). Creativity in the design process: Co-evolution of problem–solution. *Design Studies, 22*(5), 425–437.

Esser, H. (1993). The rationality of everyday behavior: A rational choice reconstruction of the theory of action by Alfred Schultz. *Rationality and Society, 5*(1), 7–31.

Feldman, M. S., & March, J. G. (1981). Information in organizations as signal and symbol. *Administrative Science Quarterly, 26,* 171–186.

Folkmann, M. N. (2010). *Enabling creativity. Imagination in design processes.* Paper presented at the proceedings of the 1st International Conference on design creativity ICDC.

Fredrickson, L. (1999). Vision and material practice: Vladimir Tatlin and the design of everyday objects. *Design Issues, 15*(1), 49–74.

Harper, D. (1987). *Working knowledge. Skill and community in a small shop.* Chicago: University of Chicago Press.

Hitzler, R. (1987). *Mundane Reflexivität: zur Verständigung mit und über Alfred Schütz.* In: Sociologia Internationalis, *25,* 143–161.

Hume, R. D. (1970). Kant and Coleridge on imagination. *The Journal of Aesthetics and Art Criticism, 28*(4), 485–496.

Ingold, T. (2013). *Making: Anthropology, archaeology, art and architecture.* New York: Routledge.

Jung, H., & Stolterman, E. (2012). *Digital form and materiality: propositions for a new approach to interaction design research.* Paper presented at the 7th Nordic Conference on human-computer interaction: Making sense through design.

Kaufman, J. C., & Baer, J. (2004). Hawking's Haiku, Madonna's Math: Why it is hard to be creative in every room of the house. In R. J. Sternberg, E. L. Grigorenko, & J. L. Singer (Eds.), *Creativity: From potential to realization.* Washington DC: American Psychological Association.

Kaufmann, G. (2006). *Hva er kreativitet? (What is creativity).* Oslo: Universitetsforlaget.

Kneller, J. (1990). Imaginative freedom and the German enlightenment. *Journal of the History of Ideas, 51*(2), 217–232.

Knoblauch, H. (1992). *Anthropologie der symbolischen Kommunikation Forschungspapier für den SFB 511 Literatur und Anthropologie.* Konstanz: University of Konstanz, GE.

Lanzara, G. F. (1983). The design process: Frames, metaphors and games. In U. Briefs, C. U. Ciborra, L. Schneider (Eds.), *Systems design for, with and by the user.* Amsterdam: North-Holland.

Lindblom, C. E. (1959). The science of "muddling through". *Public Administration Review, 19,* 79–88.

Löwgren, J., & Stolterman, E. (2007). *Thoughtful interaction design: A design perspective on information technology.* Cambridge: MIT Press.

Metcalfe, J., & Wiebe, D. (1987). Intuition in insight and noninsight problem solving. *Memory & Cognition, 15,* 238–246.

Molander, B. (1996). *Kunskap i handling (Knowledge in action).* Gothenberg: Daidalos.

Pye, D. (1964). *The nature of design.* New York: Reinhold Publishing Corporation.

Rittel, H. W., & Webber, M. M. (1973). Dilemmas in a general theory of planning. *Policy Sciences, 4*(2), 155–169.

Schön, D. A. (1983). *The reflective practitioner.* Harper Collins.

Schön, D. A. (1995). Knowing-in-action: The new scholarship requires a new epistemology. *Change: The Magazine of Higher Learning, 27*(6), 27–34.

Schütz, A. (1943). The problem of rationality in the social world. *Economica, 10*(38), 130–149.

Schütz, A. (1945). On multiple realities. *Philosophy and Phenomenological Research, 5*(4), 533–576.

Schütz, A. (1951). Choosing among projects of action. *Philosophy and Phenomenological Research, 12*(2), 161–184.

Schütz, A. (1954). Concept and theory formation in the social sciences. *The Journal of Philosophy, 51*(9), 257–273.

Schütz, A. (1962). On multiple realities. In A. Schütz (Ed.), *Collected papers I* (pp. 207–259). Den Haag: Nijhoff.

Simon, H. (1960). *The new science of managerial decision.* New York: Harper and Row.

Tellioglu, H., Wagner, I., & Lainer, R. (1998). *Open design methodologies. Exploring architectural practice for systems design.* Paper presented at the proceedings of PDC'98, Seattle.

Chapter 3
The Cases

The case descriptions in this chapter are based on reconstructing the history of both projects. When engaging with this task it became immediately clear that in both cases this reconstruction had to begin well before the official start of the project, since both were based upon and inspired by previous work that dated back several years.

In *IPCity* design work proceeded in an iterative way, in cycles of design-evaluation-redesign, with new features being added. This is why much of what we identify as design-decisions is well documented and argued in the project reports. These reports and several publications were supplemented by personal memory of the numerous disagreements that had come to the fore in project meetings and in participatory workshops with users; and of the debates of alterative ways to proceed. These personal memories also include the four review meetings where choices were questioned and alternatives suggested.

The reconstruction of the *Sisom* project is largely based on the good video documentation of the workshops with users, as well as numerous publications. As the participatory designer had been absent during parts of the design work, she engaged in additional reconstruction work with the project leader in the form of interviews, in which they also reviewed project work preceding *Sisom*.

While *IPCity* was a large and relatively open-ended project, with a duration of more than four years, involving several partner organizations, *Sisom* was much smaller and quite focused. This explains why in our analysis more material from *IPCity* is considered.

This chapter provides a brief introduction to the two cases, focusing on their chronology and on details of the participatory process. More case material will be presented then in the following chapters when we look at both projects under the aspects of decision-making, power, and participation. We have to add that the empirical material we work with is not ethnographical. We carry out what might be considered a 'secondary analysis' of written project accounts that are based on empirical material (some of it ethnographic). The personal memories contextualize this material and add details that are absent from the reports themselves, for different reasons. The nature of the empirical material also influences the narrative style of the analysis.

T. Bratteteig, I. Wagner, *Disentangling Participation,* Computer Supported
Cooperative Work, DOI 10.1007/978-3-319-06163-4_3,
© Springer International Publishing Switzerland 2014

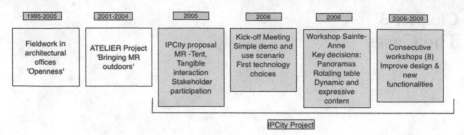

Fig. 3.1 Overview of key activities

3.1   Collaborative Urban Planning

This case is about the design of a collaborative mixed reality application, a project in which one of the authors (Ina Wagner) has been central from its initiation to its end. The application aimed to support mixed teams of urban planners, politicians, and citizens in using participatory technologies to create and manipulate design alternatives for real urban planning projects[1].

The Mixed Reality tool: the *ColorTable* turned into the centerpiece of a *Mixed Reality Tent*, for supporting on-site participatory urban design. This *MR-Tent* was part of the *IPCity* project, which lasted from 2006 to 2010. We need, however, to go some years back to include some important design decisions that happened before the official start of the project (Fig. 3.1). In the period from 1995 to 2005, Ina Wagner in several research projects had developed an understanding of architectural practice, based on years of fieldwork, where she studied architecture and urban planning in 'real settings', with a focus on collaborative practices and artifacts, their persuasive nature, their materiality, as well as their representational and coordinative functions. This ethnographic work had inspired two European research and participatory design projects: DESARTE (The computer-supported design of artifacts and spaces in architecture: landscape architecture, 1996–1997 and 1999–2001); and ATELIER (Architecture and Technologies for Inspirational Learning Environments, 2001–2004). It was the ATELIER project, which had ended with the notion of 'bringing mixed-reality technologies out of the studio' (Binder et al. 2011), which most directly inspired *IPCity*. A first vision of what these 'out of the studio' technologies could be was specified in the *IPCity* project proposal in 2005. The proposal contained the idea of the 'tent' as a portable mixed reality system, with a 'mixed-media workbench interface in support of e-painting, e-constructing, scouting, and exploring'. Hence, *IPCity* did not start with studying the work practices of urban planners: it rather built on previous fieldwork and explorations of supporting technologies, with a strong commitment to strengthening the voice of citizen in urban planning, including the conviction that this was a goal worthwhile pursuing. It was a vision-driven project.

---

[1] IPCity (FP6-2004-IST-4-27571) "Integrated Project on Interaction and Presence in Urban Environments" funded by the European Commission.

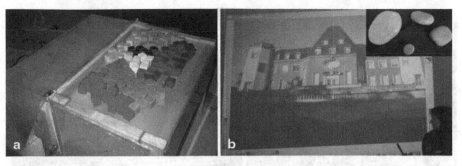

Fig. 3.2 a Tangible Image Query. **b** Coloured stones were used to create a mixed reality scene: a lake in front of the picture of a castle

3.1.1 The 'Umbrella' of a European Research Project

IPCity was a research project, which operated under the conditions of European projects regulating management procedures, budget, deliverables, deadlines, and review meetings. The *MR-Tent* was one of four so-called 'showcases', all of which were to contribute to the common theme of 'mixed-reality and presence in urban environments'. Ina Wagner acted as project leader for the 'urban planning' show-case; she was also responsible for integrating all four showcases on the theoretical and methodological level, with the idea of producing common results. She had been one of the initiators of *IPCity* and established an interdisciplinary *designer team* at Vienna University of Technology, which included in the first year Thomas Psik, later Valérie Maquil and Michal Idziorek (computer science), Lisa Ehrenstrasser (product design), Mira Wagner (visual arts), and Gammon (musician). Main partner in the collaborative urban planning showcase was the *urban planner team* of Jean-Jacques Terrin (Université Marne-de-la-Vallée), with Maria Basile, Burcu Odzdirlik, and Sevasti Vardouli, all of them with a background in architecture. Dieter Schmalstieg and Markus Sareika (Graz University of Technology) contributed with technological input and a special application *UrbanSketcher* to the showcase; Giang P. Nguyen and Hans Jørgen Andersen (Aalborg University) with the tracking algorithm (which we will explain later). For evaluating the *MR-Tent* and *ColorTable* in the context of real urban projects, the collaboration of many people was required: these ranged from the 'owners' of urban projects, such as architects, other specialists and local authorities, to 'normal' citizens as workshop participants.

3.1.2 IPCity in Brief

The *ColorTable* was to a large extent defined in the project kick-off meeting where the chief developer (at that time Thomas Psik) arranged a simple demo of a possible solution together with a scenario (Fig. 3.2). The demo was inspired by a small application: the *Tangible Image Query* that had been developed within ATELIER (Binder et al. 2011), a physical interface for browsing an image database in an interactive way.

In line with PD, the designer team decided to move this first design idea quickly out into the field, after only six months in the project. The first prototype was

Fig. 3.3 Wall scenario (*left*) and mixed reality scene (*right*)

brought into a real urban project: the redesign of the grounds of Sainte-Anne, a large psychiatric clinic in Paris. Participating users were the leading architect and hospital staff, including a professor of psychiatry at the Sorbonne. In preparing for the workshop, the whole project team (both the designers and the urban planners) spent time on understanding the urban issues at stake and developed two scenarios as well as content for participants to work with. One of these scenarios concerned the wall that encloses the hospital premises (Fig. 3.3): should the wall be removed, or partially removed, made transparent or its texture be changed; should it for example be used as a screen and exhibition space for the hospital's collection of 'art brut'? This raised questions with regard to the function of the wall: could the wall be conceived as a mediator between inside (of people, history, memory, knowledge, creation) and outside (the city, the neighbours), in addition to providing protection for patients?

The first prototype the team brought to Sainte-Anne was simple: a white cardboard spread out on a table; a set of coloured tokens of different shapes; small cards with a thumbnail representation of 'content' (images, 3D objects) and with a barcode interface; a camcorder suspended over the table; and a projector (Fig. 3.4). This first *ColorTable* prototype was modeled on a 'worlds in miniature' (WIM) approach, where the table and the color objects serve as representations of different elements of a mixed-reality world. The basic interaction consisted of picking up one of the colored objects, assigning an image or sound file using the barcode interface and placing it on the table. The composed scene could be viewed on an additional screen, showing a perspective view, while the surface of the ColorTable represented a top view of the environment, which at the time of this first workshop was only a white surface.

Workshop participants immediately started experimenting, composing mixed reality scenes, with the content being projected against an image showing a part of the wall surrounding the premises of Sainte-Anne (Fig. 3.3). Their comments paired with the team's observations provided valuable feedback, which 'pushed' the design in directions that should shape the project to the end.

Several key design decisions were taken as a result of this first workshop: to work with multiple representations of the site, including photographic panoramas for being projected on the wall; to allow for rotating and zooming the table as well as the wall panorama; to include dynamic, changeable content; and to dedicate effort on how to design the 'tangibles' (for a detailed description of these decisions see Chap. 4).

Fig. 3.4 The first 'technology probe'

In retrospect we can say that the following eight participatory workshops mainly served to implement these decisions and to improve the design. Sure, also new functionalities were conceived, evaluated and redesigned. But the *overall conc*ept of the *MR-Tent* was maintained throughout the project. Having said that, it should also be mentioned that in the course of the project some of the features of the *ColorTable* changed considerably and visibly. Just to give one example: the high number of physical objects and interaction modules of the *ColorTable* stressed the importance of organizing the workspace. All the material and devices needed, should be within reach of workshop participants but not in the way. Observations in several workshops showed that users often had trouble to organize the placement of the diverse objects. They were placed at every possible spot around the tabletop, blocking tracking and free interaction. The designer team therefore experimented with different possibilities to guide users in this spatial organization. Figure 3.5 shows two versions of the *ColorTable*.

We will later, when discussing issues of decision-making, power, and participation, bring in more examples of design changes over the course of the project, highlighting different ways of creating choices, of arriving at a decision and implementing it, as well as different degrees of participation.

On the final *ColorTable* prototype users can arrange and position tokens on physical maps of different scales, representing interventions in urban space (Fig. 3.6). A vertical projection renders the scene against different representations of the real site. Objects of the mixed-reality world can be modified and adapted in scale, transparency, colour, and offset to the ground. Users can place different types of paths animated by flows of pedestrians, cyclists, cars, a train, etc. to a scene. They define areas, and can mark them with textures. They can also create and explore the soundscape connected with the visual scene. Figure 3.7 describes the basic interactions with the final *ColorTable* prototype.

Fig. 3.5 The *ColorTable*—Organization of the workspace of the third and the fifth prototype

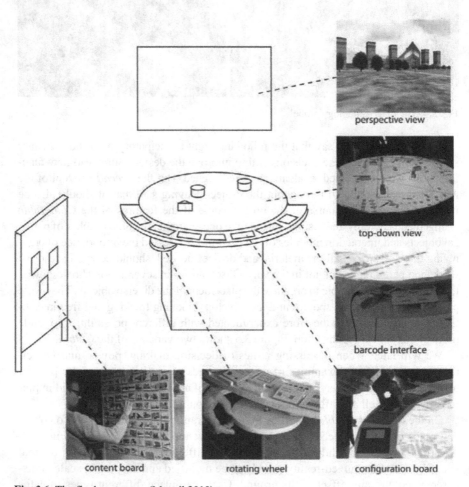

perspective view

top-down view

barcode interface

content board   rotating wheel   configuration board

Fig. 3.6 The final prototype. (Maquil 2010)

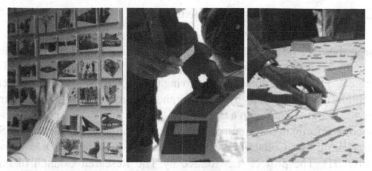

Selecting content, placing a content card on selected coloured RFID field, which associates content with colour blue, and placing blue triangle on physical map.

Manipulating content by placing a 'command card' (e.g. 'scale decrease') on colour zone of the single object to be manipulated.

Setting connections requires two rectangular tokens that define end points and angles defining curvature. Content card defines type of flow (e.g. pedestrian, high traffic) visible as moving dots on map.

Areas that are enclosed by connections can be filled with ground textures (grass, stone, water, etc.) by simply placing a circular token, the colour of which has been associated with a particular texture in the area on the map.

Turning the wooden wheel to a) rotate view or b) zoom while checking with gaze at projection.

Freeze scene, upload previous scene with barcode interface.

Fig. 3.7 Basic interactions with *ColorTable* interface. (Wagner 2011)

3.2   Collaborative Symptom Assessment

This case is about the design of a mobile information system for patients in hospital settings. One of the authors (Tone Bratteteig) was actively involved in the PD parts of this project. The system aimed at improving the communication between chronically ill children and clinicians by allowing the children to register symptoms and problems ahead of meeting with a doctor.

The mobile information system: *Sisom*, was developed in The Centre for Shared Decision Making and Collaborative Care Research (CSDM) at Oslo University Hospital (OUH). The project was funded by The Research Council of Norway (RCN) in collaboration with *OUH*, and lasted from 2005 to 2007. Since 2007 the *Sisom* system has been in pilot use in two hospital units, and *CSDM* has further developed the system for more patient groups (heart diseases in addition to cancer).

The history of the *Sisom* project started well before 2005, in the late 1990s when Cornelia Ruland did her PhD. She was educated as a pediatric nurse and her PhD focused on communication problems of patients and clinicians with a particular emphasis on children. Children have difficulties communicating well with adults about how they feel when ill and therefore often receive less adequate treatment and care. Ruland's idea was to design a computer-based system containing all known symptoms for a specific diagnosis, collected from medical publications (evidence-based), systematized and categorized with the help of experts and patients, and presented to the patient before his/her consultation with a clinician. This would enable the patient to give more and better information about all symptoms, and hence a more complete picture of his/her situation. Ruland engaged in developing a number of prototypes to concretize the idea: on a PC in 1999, on a Palm Pilot in 2000, on a tablet computer in 2001 (Fig. 3.8).

In 2002 Ruland was hired to establish and lead the CSDM and initiated a project to develop *Choice*: *Creating better Health Outcomes by Improving Communication about Patients' Experiences*. The *Choice* system has been used by cancer patients in three wards at *OUH*, since 2003.

3.2.1   Sisom: The Idea

In 2005 Ruland initiated the development of a children's version of the *Choice* system. Ruland was the project leader, collaborating with some of the people at CSDM: Torun Vatne: a child psychologist doing her PhD, and systems developers Roar Andersen and Denis Pokotylyuk. She also contacted Tone Bratteteig at the Department of Informatics (IFI), University of Oslo (UiO), who joined the team with her colleague Christina Mörtberg and the master students: Elisabeth Moe, Valemon Sending, Rune Hoel and Simon Sigurdson Hjelle. Just as the project activities started up (May 2005) a graphical designer was hired, and later in the autumn a Flash developer also joined the group.

The aims and scope of the *Sisom* system were set by the precursor *Choice*: it was supposed to be used in the same way. Some requirements were therefore established

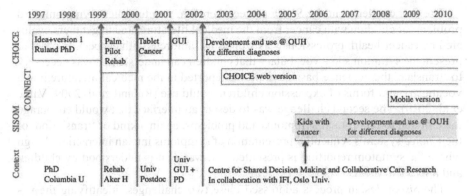

Fig. 3.8 Overview of key activities

very early. The system should fit into the workflow of the hospital. It should be possible to use in a variety of situations, mainly waiting rooms (before a doctor's appointment) and in the ward (when hospitalized and in bed); patients should be able to take the system with them when moving around; but also use it when staying in bed, getting intravenous medication, when hands are plastered, etc. Hence, the system should be easy to use. A touch sensitive screen was chosen because it does not require a flat surface (like using a mouse requires), and a pen-based interaction was chosen because it seems that children can perform 'point-and-click' interaction easily and quickly compared to 'drag-and-drop'. As the technical platform a tablet with an 8.9" screen was chosen, with enough computing power and memory to enable easy development.

Sisom was also content-wise framed by the *Choice* system. Both systems allow patients to report symptoms and problems on a computer system ahead of an appointment with a clinician. The *Choice* system leads the user through a sequence of categories of problems and symptoms tailored to this particular patient group. In this way more symptoms are reported and dealt with. Ruland et al. have documented that patients using *Choice* receive better treatment and care because more symptoms and problems are addressed. As a result, their stay in the hospital is generally shorter. The *Sisom* project started out as children's *Choice* ('ped's *Choice*'), motivated by the fact that children express their symptoms in ways that are different from adults. Similar to the *Choice* system, the overall aim is to enable health care personnel to get more knowledge about the child's health situation.

3.2.2 Sisom in Brief

Sisom is designed to help children age 7–12 with cancer to identify and report their symptoms/problems in a child-friendly, age-adjusted manner, and assist clinicians (nurses and physicians) in addressing and integrating children's reported symptoms and problems in their patient care.

The first challenge in the *Sisom* project therefore was to collect symptoms and problems of children with cancer from the medical literature, and to get them evaluated by cancer health professionals as well as by children (with cancer). In order to present the symptoms in a vocabulary that children can understand it was necessary to 'translate' the evidence-based symptoms reported in the medical literature into a vocabulary and forms of expression children would use (Ruland et al. 2009; Vatne et al. 2010). The second challenge was to design an interface that would encourage the children to report their symptoms and problems, again a kind of 'translation' of the *Choice* system's sequential presentation of symptoms into an interaction design where the symptom reporting is presented in a way that is understood by children and appeals to them.

The *Sisom* design process addressed these two challenges: identifying the vocabulary and designing a user interface that would appeal to children. Planning the work for the latter challenge was inspired by Allison Druin's method for participatory design with children (Druin 2002).

3.2.2.1 Evidence-Based Collection of Symptoms

During the first phase of *Sisom* the project leader (Ruland) and the psychologist collected symptoms and problems of children with cancer reported in the literature. A preliminary list of symptoms and problems was abstracted from the literature for potential inclusion. Next, they conducted a series of focus group discussions with clinical specialists in pediatric oncology (physicians, nurses, psychologists, social workers) who critically reviewed the preliminary symptom list for relevance, comprehensibility, completeness, and level of detail. The focus groups resulted in some revisions of the list based on their expert opinion. The last step was to have the list reviewed by six parents of children with cancer. In addition to being asked to evaluate the symptom list according to the same criteria as the clinicians, the parents were also requested to pay particular attention to whether or not the symptoms and problems on the list were expressed in a simple, understandable, non-medical lay language that children could understand. They were also asked what terms and expressions children used when communicating about symptoms with them. This resulted in some further revisions specifically of symptom wordings.

The result of this phase was a list of evidence-based symptoms, refined and modified by cancer professionals at OUH and parents of children with cancer. The list of symptoms is the basis of *Sisom*, and addressing the first challenge.

3.2.2.2 Participatory Design of the User Interface

The second challenge, designing a user interface that would appeal to children was addressed by organizing a PD process with children. A pilot session with children of CSDM employees was arranged to try out the workshop format with children and also to get more familiar with the format (Fig. 3.9).

The project leader and the psychologist recruited children from a nearby school to the project. Two boys and four girls from 4th grade and three girls and three boys from

Fig. 3.9 Pilot design session. (Sending 2006)

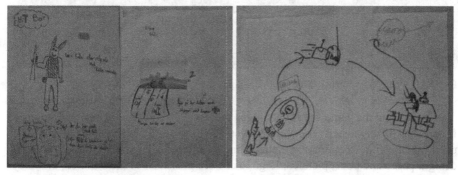

Fig. 3.10 Drawings of interaction mechanisms inspired by games. Left to right: 'hit boy' shoots at the places that hurt, car race: drive where it hurts. (Sending 2006); a game-like collection of needs as a way to go to the next level. (Moe 2006)

6th grade were recruited and participated in the PD sessions, in their age groups. A sequence of four design sessions was carried out with each of the age groups, where the project leader and the psychologist acted as facilitators. The IFI team participated in all the sessions as observers and in some cases also as facilitators.

All design sessions were videotaped and documented. The material from the sessions consists of 22 hours of videotape, observation notes and the low-tech prototypes that were developed. The material was analysed and discussed by the interdisciplinary *Sisom* team, including health professionals, a child psychologist, a child educational therapist, programmers, and designers. The aim of the analysis was to identify children's contributions and ideas as well as their roles and interactions in the design process.

3.2.2.3   Games as Genre

The first session presented the children with a small selection of games, including a game designed for children with cancer (leukaemia) (Fig. 3.10). For each child an observer watched and took notes while a facilitator interviewed them about their experiences.

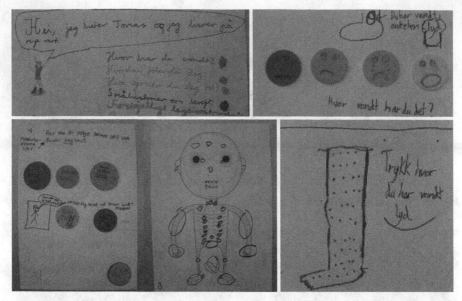

Fig. 3.11 Where does it hurt? (Moe 2006; Sending 2006)

After testing the game, the psychologist told a story about a child who had stomach flu and had to stay in bed. The children were asked to design a tablet PC that could be used by this child to express symptoms and problems. A large selection of tools for design: paper and pens, pictures, Lego, etc. were presented to the children, and they sat down to draw interfaces and parts of the interaction. The session ended with the children explaining their ideas and discussing them with each other (Fig. 3.11).

3.2.2.4   Drawing the User Interface

The second session started with a new story about a child with an injury and some problems, who could get help by telling about the problems using a computer. The children continued to work on the drawings they had worked on in the previous session. The ideas were evaluated in terms of how they fit with the goals of *Sisom*, general pedagogical principles and usability criteria for children.

This time some new materials were introduced: some drawings made by the graphic designer based on ideas from the previous session. In this way adults helped form design ideas. The adults showed interface and navigation examples to the children and in this way the children became more aware of what was possible and wanted. The children included the figures in their own work (Fig. 3.12).

However, children design differently from adults—they are not professional designers and do not always make designs that follow an adult logic. They may, for instance, spend a whole session on details like drawing flowers in the background landscape or on how to select eye and hair colour for the *Sisom* main figure. The organization of the design process was based on the view that the ambition to design for ill children requires knowledge and insights based on pedagogy, psychology and clinical experience that children themselves do not have. Moreover, in a project that

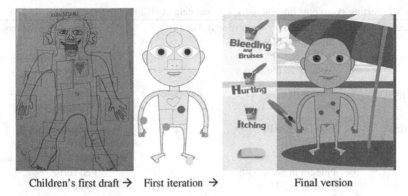

Children's first draft →   First iteration →   Final version

Fig. 3.12 The session ended with explanations of the children's sketches and prototypes. (Ruland et al. 2008)

aims at a product the goals and pre-defined criteria of the hospital needed to be addressed: it was important to ensure that the resulting software could help children report their symptoms and problem experiences, without being too time-consuming or challenging. Not all of the children's ideas were therefore seen as feasible: they were fun and time-consuming (funny noises, vivid animations for a symptom e.g., throwing up). Even when reminded that they were not designing a game, the children many times returned to game-like designs.

3.2.2.5   Children's Categorization of Symptoms

The third session was a card sorting session aimed at finding out how the children categorized and classified the symptoms to be used in the system. The card sorting exercise was tested with children of CSDM employees first.

The cards had words on them that the project leader and the psychologist had prepared on the basis of the vocabulary from the first phase of the project. The card sorting was done in two rounds. In the first round everyday words were sorted into categories (Table 3.1). The second round focused on matching symptoms to problems and explaining why for example a hurting stomach can be a symptom connected to rather different situations: difficult school days, fear of the future, medication causing nausea. The facilitators assisted by reading out loud the cards and explaining their meaning (when the children did not understand them).

3.2.2.6   Prototyping in a Real Life Setting

In the fourth session the use situation was in focus. The facilitators had provided a hospital bed and had dressed as health care workers. In each of the age groups one of the children volunteered to lie in bed and simulate an injury (arm bandage) while the others gathered around the bed. The child, who was in bed, tried out a few prototypes designed by the Master students. In addition they tried the (adult) *Choice* system (Fig. 3.13).

Table 3.1 Sorting symptoms into categories. (Bratteteig et al. 2010)

Physical problem	Cry a lot (own suggestions)	Tired	Sleep during the day
	Bleed nose-blood		Easily tried
	Broken leg		Don't manage anthing
	Wounds on the skin		Cannot read
Head pain	Head ache	Emotions	Afraid
	Dizzy		Nightmares
Vomiting	Pain in the belly		Embarrassed
	Vomit		Angry
	Nausea		Miss family and friends
	Phlegm in my mouth		Fell sorry
	Things smell bad/ unpleasant		Cry a lot
	Nose feels tight		Irritated
	Cough	Medication problems	Can't take my medicine
	Warm or sweat		Don't want to play with others
Mouth problems	Dry in the mouth		Shivering hands
	Pain in the mouth		Difficult to walk
	Don't manage to eat	Medication problems	Can't take my medicine
			Disgusting to take medicine

Fig. 3.13 Testing the prototype. (Bratteteig et al. 2010)

After the test the children discussed how they experienced the system and prototypes. The discussion turned into a more open and general conversation about what kinds of ideas would work for children in bed. The children agreed that the application needs to balance an engaging, child-friendly interface with the 'serious' nature of the task and should not be perceived as a game: it turned out that they actually preferred the *Choice* system to the game-like prototypes. To the adults, it was important that the system should not tempt children to select symptoms just because their pictures or interactions are fun to watch, if they do not reflect how the child experiences the actual symptoms. However, an important feature of the *Choice* and *Sisom* systems is to lead the patient through the whole list in order to cover all

Fig. 3.14 The final prototype. (Ruland et al. 2008)

relevant symptoms. In addition, the system needs to be engaging so that the children want to use it. A real balancing act!

3.2.2.7   User Testing

The final phase of the design process concerned the development and testing of high-fidelity prototypes of (some of) the children's ideas, with this balancing act in mind. The prototyping took time and an extra Flash designer was employed. In order to keep up the speed the project leader decided to develop only one prototype.

The prototype (Fig. 3.14) was tested first with children (two boys and two girls) of CSDM employees—the same children who had participated in the pilot drawing and card sorting sessions. The project leader acted as facilitator and the psychologist as observer during the testing, encouraging the children to think aloud during the test. Finally the prototype was tested with two children with cancer, a boy 11 years old and a girl, 8 years old. Only the project leader was present and acted as a facilitator in order to not make the children too tired. After this testing, the *Sisom* system was developed and tested in real use in the cancer ward.

3.3   Summary

IPCity and *Sisom* are PD projects, each with a participatory result that reflected the project vision. However, the contexts of both projects were rather different; so were their scope and the participatory processes. The *ColorTable* developed into a highly complex tool with many functionalities: the ambition was to support users in addressing the whole range of urban issues in a project, with openness and immediacy as key elements. *Sisom* focused on a well-circumscribed objective: to help sick children report on the symptoms they experienced, thereby giving them a voice in consultations with health care personnel. The tool had to be engaging, very simple, and easy to integrate into the workflow in a hospital. These differences in how the two projects were framed had implications for decision-making, as we will show in the next chapter.

References

Binder, T., Ehn, P., Jacucci, G., De Michelis, G., Linde, P., & Wagner, I. (2011). *Design things*. Cambridge: MIT Press.

Bratteteig, T., Wagner, I., Morrison, A., Stuedahl, D., & Mörtberg, C. (2010). Research practices in digital design. In I. Wagner, T. Bratteteig, & D. Stuedahl (Eds.), *Exploring digital design* (pp. 17–54). London: Springer.

Druin, A. (2002). The role of children in the design of new technology. *Behaviour and Information Technology, 21*(1), 1–25.

Maquil, V. (2010). *The ColorTable: An interdisciplinary design process*. Wien: Vienna University of Technology.

Moe, E. Y. (2006). *Evaluation of children's usability criteria*. (Master thesis), Oslo University.

Ruland, C. M., et al. (2013). Effects of an internet support system to assist cancer patients in reducing symptom distress: A randomized controlled trial. *Cancer Nursing, 36*(1), 6–17.

Ruland, C. M., Hamilton, G. A., & Schjødt-Osmo, B. (2009). The complexity of symptoms and problems experienced in children with cancer: A review of the literature. *Journal of Pain and Symptom management, 37*(3), 403–418.

Ruland, C. M., Starren, J., & Vatne, T. M. (2008). Participatory design with children in the development of a support system for patient-centered care in pediatric oncology. *Journal of Biomedical Informatics, 41*(4), 624–635.

Sending, V. A. (2006). *En kvalitativ undersøkelse av elementer som motiverer barn til å bruke et diagnostiseringssystem*. (Master thesis), Oslo University.

Vatne, T. M., Slaugther, S., & Ruland, C. M. (2010). How children with cancer communicate and think about symptoms. *Journal of pediatric oncology nursing, 27*(1), 24–32.

Wagner, I. (2011). Building urban narratives: Collaborative site-seeing and envisioning in the MR Tent. *Computer Supported Cooperative Work (CSCW), 21*(1), 1–42.

Chapter 4
Kinds of Decisions

The first step in our analysis is to identify some of the decisions made in the two projects. We introduce several distinctions here, which we find useful: decisions on values and concepts; decisions on how to implement the vision; and decisions requiring negotiations with the outside world. The 'kinds of decisions' we distinguish reflect relevance or weight of a decision, as well as aspects of the design process. Hence, the distinctions are heuristic and practical rather than based on a theory.

4.1 Kinds of Decisions: The Case of Urban Planning

When it comes to *who* took the decisions in *IPCity*, we found that different participants made different kinds of decisions. The project was led by the Austrian *designer team*, which had a strong commitment to participation and expertise in ethnography, interaction and product design, computer graphics, visual arts, sound design, as well as fieldwork experience in architecture. The participatory designer in the Austrian team had full authority as the project leader. The French *urban planner team* was equally important in the project vision and acted as co-designers and 'expert users', selecting the sites, defining the urban issues at stake, negotiating participation with local authorities, and mobilizing their network of colleagues. This third group represented the 'outside world' of stakeholders in urban planning, with whom an agreement had to be found for the core events of the project: participatory workshops in the context of real urban planning workshops. A fourth group were the *workshop participants*, a heterogeneous set of stakeholders with different competences and interests that varied from workshop to workshop. Important to add that the course of the project as a whole was influenced by the yearly review meetings organized by the funding agency, in which four reviewers voiced their criticism and defined additional, or from the point of view of the project team, sometimes also controversial objectives for the next working period.

T. Bratteteig, I. Wagner, *Disentangling Participation,* Computer Supported
Cooperative Work, DOI 10.1007/978-3-319-06163-4_4,
© Springer International Publishing Switzerland 2014

4.1.1   Decisions on Values and Concepts

The vision for the project is the result of many years of collaboration of the participatory designer with architects and urban planners. The main vision was grounded
in almost ten years of fieldwork in architectural offices and constituted the basis for
the collaboration between the Austrian and the French team.

4.1.1.1   Openness

The participatory designer brought a strong commitment in the form of the notion of 'openness' as constitutive of creative (architectural) design into the project.
Openness implies systematically cultivating the 'art of seeing'; engaging with a
plethora of materials, inspirational resources as well as material conceptualizations
of a design concept; being able to work in a 'meandering' way, with 'floating concepts' and 'placeholders', while maintaining things at different stages of incomple-
tion (Lainer and Wagner 1998). Openness in the context of an urban project also is
to do with giving space to the multiplicity of perspectives and to ambiguity of what
a possible solution could be.

    The commitment to openness inspired many aspects of the *MR-Tent*, in particular
the idea to develop a 'new language' that would enable all the participants in an
urban project to collaborate on addressing urban issues and expressing their vision.
The project team early on agreed upon not developing a simulation tool in order to
maintain that the design decisions were the responsibility of the participants in an
urban project. The floor would be theirs with regard to what they wanted to do and
which level of complexity they wanted to address.

4.1.1.2   Stakeholder Participation

The second strong commitment was to designing participatory technologies for urban planning that could invite real stakeholders to the design table. This was an
idea that also appealed to the French urban planner team in the project, although
their thinking about and experiences with participation differed considerably from
the PD tradition. They based their arguments in favour of participation in the increasing complexity of political, economic, and social demands, as well as in the
large number of stakeholders implicated in urban design, each of them representing
diverse professional cultures, academic training, and economic logics (e.g., Callon
et al. 2001). Their problem was to understand what lay people could contribute to
an urban project, which is by definition complex and large-scale, involving myriads
of open issues. This conflict came to the fore already in one of the first workshops
where we were able to observe two different groups working with the *ColorTable*.
One, guided by the chief architect for Sainte-Anne, worked with a precise intervention. Her approach to participation was to carefully prepare scenes, selecting the
appropriate content, so that participants only got 'to have a variation of very small
things'. The other group worked more with stories and ideas about activities. They

saw the technologies 'as eventually opening up a space for mutual learning (in their words: 'apprentissage collective'), having different stakeholders exploring and confronting ideas. They stressed the value of engaging in activities that are different from what they termed the 'ritual space of creating a program' ('l'espace rituel de programmation') (Maquil et al. 2007, p. 73).

The decision in favor of giving the floor to lay participants conflicted with a strong expert tradition. However, not all the urban specialists that participated in the *MR-Tent* workshops claimed a 'privileged voice'. As one of them expressed it, the *ColorTable* helped participants to 'not discuss in a confrontational way'. Building something together made them positive, but it took a long learning process and required relatively mature technologies for the urban specialists to really 'see' that all participants in the *MR-Tent* addressed 'serious' urban issues and made valuable contributions. Although participation in urban planning has some tradition (e.g., Al-Kodmany 1999), it is not common practice.

4.1.1.3 Immediacy

Connected to the vision of openness and stakeholder participation was the idea to support the *ad-hoc creation* of urban mixed reality scenes. This immediacy was made possible by the decision to not develop 'simulation tools' that support 'realism' but instead emphasize imagination and exploration. It was precisely this decision to support the *ad-hoc creation* of mixed reality scenes that made working in the *MR-Tent* different from other tabletop applications in support of urban planning (e.g., Arias et al. 2000). The implications of this approach for the design of the *MR Tent* were not clear at the beginning of the project and were also in parts contested by the urban planner team. The tool worked against the expectations of many architects and urban planners to achieve a high degree of 'precision'. This became clear, for example, in the third participatory workshop where we focused on urban sound. The team's approach to sound was qualitative and 'atmospheric' and the invited urban sound specialist was irritated that, for example, placing a large building in between her hearing position and the street did not dampen the sound. A long and heated debate started between the urban planners and the designer team about how 'realistic' the mixed reality scenes needed to be to 'carry conviction'.

In the end of the project the urban planning team made a strong argument in favor of the overall approach we had chosen, emphasizing that the possibility for building on everybody's imagination in a real time design-in-the-making process 'seems to empower the participants and allows full cycles of discussion to be put in place' (Maquil et al. 2010, p. 117).

4.1.1.4 Urban concepts

What had an enormous influence on the project was the joint work of both teams on issues of representation. How to represent an urban project moved to the foreground with the urban planner team defining 'urban issues', such as scale, borders, ambi-

Fig. 4.1 Examples of 'urban concepts': scale (upper left), mobility (upper right), time (below)

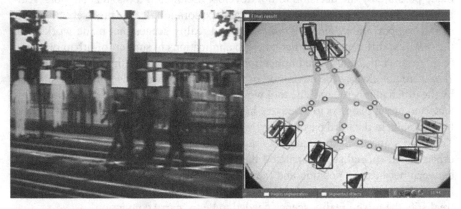

Fig. 4.2 First instantiation of flows (left); curved paths and flows visible on the table map, final prototype (right)

ence, mobility, time, etc. (Fig. 4.1). They also provided visual examples for each of these issues, which were discussed in the team. These urban issues moved into the foreground and drove the decisions on functionalities to be developed.

One of these decisions was to include dynamic content thereby supporting the discussion of issues of mobility. Flows—of people, bicycles and cars—were introduced. Fig. 4.2. (left) shows a first instantiation of this idea. In the panorama we can see flows of blue people; they animate the space and bring a human dimension into the mixed reality scene. We can even see them mix with real people who are passing by outside. The final prototype (Fig. 4.2. right) allows for curved paths and different types of flows.

4.1.2   Decisions on How to Implement The Vision

Our next kind of design decisions—how to implement the vision –, were taken rather early on and turned out to have implications that were not clear at that time. These decisions were mainly 'technical'.

4.1.2.1   Haptic Engagement: Working With Tokens

The decision to develop a tangible user interface was grounded in a strong and shared research interest of the designer team, and strengthened by hiring a product designer. The assumption was that a participatory tool with a tangible user interface and in the form of a 'round table' would foster collaboration.

The *ColorTable* uses objects—tokens—of different sizes, shapes and colors. It was inspired by the *Token and Constraints (TAC)* paradigm (Shaer 2004), which describes a relationship between a token, its variable and one or more constraints as a model of how to link physical and digital objects.

Working with 'abstract' tokens fitted well with the notion of openness. It also had unforeseen implications, moving the design of tokens, content cards, workflow and workspace into the foreground. Already at the first workshop in Sainte-Anne it became clear that the workflow was too complicated and that the table became cluttered with 'tangibles' within a short time, making it impossible to maintain order (e.g., Maquil et al. 2010). In the course of the project the designer team experimented with the design of the tokens as well as with different methods to support the basic interaction. Fig 4.3. shows three stages of the interface for selecting a color (bar code; RFID separate and integrated with the table).

Neither the urban planner team nor the workshop participants took great interest in these issues apart from welcoming these improvements.

4.1.2.2   Tracking Framework

The decision to use color came with the technical challenge to use color tracking—itself a decision. Using colored tokens offered several advantages: they are easy to prototype; the color of the physical object already provides a name or identifier for the virtual object easy to share for the participants; they are easy to understand, invite participation, and are sufficiently neutral so as not to privilege particular perspectives onto an urban project—one participant expressly talked about the color objects as 'thinking tools'.

However, computer vision algorithms based on color cannot provide the same amount of precision as for instance optical markers. Moreover, color recognition is highly sensitive to light conditions. The designer team argued for color tracking as 'a compromise between how people like to work and what computers can do, in this case opting for supporting the free positioning of graspable color objects on a map' (Maquil et al. 2008). The tracking framework developed into a complex tool

Fig. 4.3 Different designs of color selection

detecting shapes and their orientation and providing possibilities for calibration of colors and positions, but the sensitivity to changing lighting conditions remained a problem. The interactions and workflow strongly depend upon how well objects are recognized. While workshop participants were 'in general very patient and willingly waited for the tracking framework to correctly detect the tokens' and 'they adapted their behaviour with respect to the tracking framework', color tracking remained a 'weak spot' (Maquil 2010).

4.1.2.3   Bringing MR Outdoors

Another topic was the need for a shelter—the *MR Tent* (Fig. 4.4), with its own requirements: it had to be affordable (it turned out to be very expensive), robust, in compliance with building regulations, easy to transport and easy to set up, and its design had to help stabilize the lighting conditions that were crucial for the whole technical set-up. This is a complex story in itself. Conceptually the decision-process was similar to the one regarding the tracking framework: more resources than planned had to be allocated to the construction of the tent and numerous technical problems had to be mastered before it could actually be used. But the decision was and had to be maintained, since 'bringing MR outdoors' was at the core of the project vision.

Fig. 4.4 The MR Tent is a portable lab for using Mixed Reality in urban planning on location

4.1.2.4 Panoramas as Representations of the Site

At the workshop in Sainte-Anne participants immediately pointed at the limitations of a static representation: they wanted to be able to 'walk' in the projection and change perspective. This led to the idea to enable rotating the table in combination with a static panorama or a real time video image. In the photographic panorama, the viewer stands in the center, turning his/her body and gaze in a circle. Later in the project, a wheel for rotating and zooming replaced the rotating table.

The decision to work with photographic panoramas, rather than a 3D model of a site, entailed numerous other unforeseen decisions. At the second workshop in Saint-Anne the leading architect, one of the workshop participants, stressed the importance of visualizing volume and scale, as measured against the human body, so as to get a feeling for the impact of an intervention. She also defined the ability to engage with the stages of depth, placing objects, for example, behind the wall as a must (Maquil et al. 2007). The designer team used a depth map to define distances of individual objects and experimented with a height map as shape information of the floor.

Creating photographic panoramas from different viewpoints for the workshops also involved a set of choices: which points would offer good views onto the site; do they represent important vistas for people living there in the future, moving around?

When preparing for a workshop the urban planner team spent time on selecting those viewpoints. Much effort was spent then by the designer team on editing the panoramas so as to provide space for interventions, e.g. removing a building that will be replaced or cutting out trees that impede a free view onto important parts of a site but still preserving the characteristics of the real place (Fig. 4.5). Editing is a

Fig. 4.5 Edited panorama *Pontoise* workshop with parts of trees removed to provide vistas and space for interventions

highly subjective endeavor similar to film cutting; through editing the artist in the designer team took decisions, in collaboration with the urban planners, on what to make visible, thereby shaping the participants' perception of the site. This editing turned out to be one of the key design decisions that had to be taken in preparing for the participatory workshops, framing the workshops.

Participants were offered multiple representations of the site to work with, the most important being physical maps of different scales, panoramas taken from different viewpoints and a real time video stream produced by a fixed and a mobile camera. This decision reflected the practice of urban planning, which traditionally works with different views and perspectives. We much later understood how this design decision allowed participants to use representations for different purposes: planning, performing an intervention, looking from above or far away, capturing the ambience of the site' (Wagner 2011, p. 37).

4.1.2.5 Developing a 'New' Visual Language

Views on what this 'new language' should be differed. As already mentioned, the decision to work with photographic panoramas conflicted with some of the architectural tradition of creating representations, such as the need for 'precision'. It limited the degree of precision with which objects could be positioned at a correct scale and with the perception of distances. Another controversial issue was how 'realistic' the content the project team prepared for workshop participants to work with should be. In the designer team the idea prevailed to provide more expressive types of content of an inspirational quality.

This content was selected on the basis of analyzing the urban project and defining the themes to address. Participants themselves contributed to the content: some of them brought their own 'inspirational material' to the preparatory meeting in the form of cultural probes interviews (Bratteteig and Wagner 2012b) and all of them evoked themes of importance to them (Fig. 4.6). The project team then searched for content that might express these themes. The content was not 'just' the material to construct a scenography from. It was meant to evoke not only future uses of the site but qualities and ambiences.

The Vienna and French teams understood rather soon that 3D content, although important for visualizing volumes, had its limitations. They had started with simpli-

Fig. 4.6 Collection of 2D objects meant to stimulate alternative views of a site (Oslo workshop)

Fig. 4.7 Working with space as narrative; defining the way that 2D content is perceived and approached

fied versions of architectural models and ended up with simple colored building blocks. They realized that for conveying 'telling detail' and creating ambience 2D objects were needed. They support the construction of narrative on top of an architectural intervention. The 2D content the team provided was based on photographic images, sketches, architectural renderings, and paintings. To lend them a spatial dimension these images had to be cut out and 'abstracted' so that they no longer appear as flat canvasses. The visual artist found a way of lending them some 'volume' so that they still could be seen when participants rotated the panorama (Fig. 4.7). In general, she searched for images with dynamic spatial compositions, which for example had been taken from an angle or showed distinct dark-light patterns. She increased the color saturation to produce a sense of volume and depth, softened the edges, and so forth.

Fig. 4.8 Unusual representations (Oslo workshop)

Content production soon turned out to become a major issue of conflict within the project team, with different visual cultures and aesthetic experiences clashing. 'How to represent urban issues' turned out a question that did not lend itself to easy consensus. Moreover, the rich expressive content was not used as extensively as the designer team had expected, with participants only opening up to such content when they felt 'in utopia', as one of them stated (Bratteteig und Wagner 2012b). Also visual experience seemed to play a role, determining how much participants were able to 'abstract' from the specificity of the content, handling it as standing for particular 'qualities' (Fig. 4.8). One approach to these problems was to provide workshop participants with a simple application that allowed them produce their own sketches of objects they wanted to include in a scene.

4.1.2.6 Working with Sound

Working with sound was already mentioned in the project proposal (without any further specifications) and sound was part of the first workshop in Sainte-Anne. As sound is clearly an important aspect of urban environments, the urban planning team supported this decision and also took an active part in the sound research that was started, including interviews with sound specialists. Moreover, open source software (*Ambisonics*) was available.

As sound as part of urban mixed reality is a complex medium to work with, this design decision grew into a central concern in the project and required much preparation. It was decided to connect each panorama with its 'natural sound'; to offer participants the opportunity to connect visual objects with specific sounds; and to link the animated flows with their characteristic sound. This resulted in a highly complex soundscape, which workshop participants liked but did not use as actively as they worked with the visual material. The decision to allocate more resources to sound research also needed to be defended against the reviewers that did not see much value in the sound aspect of the *ColorTable*.

The team could clearly demonstrate in the end, how sound strengthened immersion into a mixed reality scene; how it contributed to the experience of spatial transformations and evoked ambiences. But the team was not able to carry this design decision to a solution that could be appropriated as freely in a collaborative way as the visual components of the *ColorTable*.

4.1.3 Decisions Requiring Negotiations with the Outside World

Being committed to PD, the designer team had insisted from the very beginning on developing and evaluating the *MR-Tent* in the context of real urban projects with real stakeholders. Nobody was at that point fully aware of what this would entail. This was to be the most 'dramatic' decision in terms of workload and potential for conflict.

For each new workshop the urban planner team had to find a suitable project and negotiate access. This turned out to be a highly political issue: local authorities had to be ensured that the project would not be intrusive and disrespectful of decisions already taken. Negotiating the legitimate participants proved to be highly sensitive. It was almost impossible to freely select participants according to our own criteria to include as many different voices as possible. Fears of criticism and opposing views had to be managed.

In addition, there was a huge amount of practical issues to be tackled. We needed permits to set up the *MR Tent*, which had to comply with local regulations concerning stability of the construction and fire protection. Transporting, setting up the tent and protecting it during the night were additional practical issues to be resolved.

The other part of necessary arrangements concerned understanding the urban issues at stake, defining scenarios and preparing the specific content needed: physical maps of different scales had to be organized and adapted (i.e. simplified); panoramas had to be taken and edited, measurements for depth-maps taken; content cards to work with had to be designed and appropriate visualizations be found and edited; and the agenda and plan for the workshop had to be developed.

Another issue was motivating and preparing workshop participants. It took the designer team almost two years before the urban planner team accepted the necessity of planning for more intense user engagement and to convince them that all participants, even the urban specialists that were invited, needed preparation. There was the practical issue of temporal commitment (who would be willing to spend at least two full days for a workshop?) and preparing for the workshop. In preparation of two of these later workshops, cultural probes were distributed two months before and used for individual interviews with each of the participants to help them develop their own vision; in the case of the third workshop, participants were invited to work in small groups (with traditional methods) on their ideas a month before engaging with the technologies. This helped them express their knowledge, experiences and interests and supported the construction of scenarios in the *MR-Tent*.

4.2   Kinds of Decisions: The Case of Collaborative Symptom Assessment

The number of people participating in the *Sisom* project was large and unstable, with several groups being only loosely connected to (parts of) the project. This organization of the project resulted in a small and stable group of people taking many of the decisions. Many people contributed and had their voices heard, but it was the *project leader* and her *core team* members *who* made the actual decisions. The project leader had full authority. As future users of the *Sisom* the *professional hospital workers* (medical doctors and nurses) were important and contributed to framing the system—with the right information as well as the right functions—so as to make it fit with the hospital routines. The second main user group, *the sick children*, did not participate in the design and were represented by healthy *children*, giving voice to children's logic and preferences. The sick children were 'represented' by reported symptoms from medical journals and the professional hospital workers. The *informatics researchers (and students)* had smaller parts in the larger project choreography, but influenced the design as well as the PD processes. Finally *the hospital* context framed the project in a number of ways, both before and after the project.

4.2.1   Decisions on Values and Concepts

The first kind of decisions to discuss is the big decisions that were not questioned during the project. They were all based on the vision for the project, which was the result of the project leader's PhD and her work as a pediatric nurse. She had defined the problem: children are not heard in meetings with health care professionals, and her solution was a support for children to make their voice more comprehensible to doctors.

4.2.1.1   A Tool for the Doctor-Patient Meeting

The inspiration for the project was the existing *Choice* system (Ruland et al.2003), already used in the hospital by adult patients to record their symptoms before seeing the doctor. *Choice* had been tested and had proven to improve the patient's conversations with the doctor as well as the treatment: the patients had faster recovery and shorter stay as well as fewer re-visits to the hospital. The vision for *Sisom* was a child-version of *Choice* aiming at giving the doctor more and better information about the patient in order to provide better care and treatment.

The original vision was to have a child use *Sisom* right before an appointment with a doctor so that a systematic recording of symptoms could be presented to the doctor. The vision can be seen as a participatory objective: as a wish to strengthen a particularly weak party in a collaborative situation. *Sisom* could give the child a stronger voice by acting as an 'ally' speaking for the child in a more comprehensible way, possibly changing the conversation between the child and the doctor to become more participative.

The strong commitment to the original vision excluded other uses of the planned system: the solution was set and not open for discussion. The project leader arranged for the participatory researcher to carry out fieldwork in the child oncology ward at the hospital. The fieldwork included observations and open interviews of patients, their parents and hospital staff in the ward. The observations included hanging out and talking with the children at the playroom/computer room and in the school rooms, sitting in the ward room and the nurses' computer room, as well as observations in cross-disciplinary morning meetings, meetings between patients (and their parents) and doctors, and meetings with hospital workers with patients in the everyday routines in the ward. The meetings between patients and doctors were of course very stressful for the patients and their parents although the doctors (and nurses) were marvelously empathetic and mindful of the situation. It seemed obvious that the moment right before a doctor's appointment is not the best time for the patients to remember all symptoms and reflect on their situation—actually the long time spans between these meetings are more susceptible to symptom registration. However, the project leader was not interested in any insight that the researcher had come to base on her fieldwork.

4.2.1.2   Translation

Taking *Choice* as a starting point defined the design challenge to be a translation problem: translating the adult symptom registration system to one suitable for children. Both the vocabulary and the interaction were seen as inappropriate for children. *Choice* is a form-based system leading the adult through a sequence of symptoms known to be relevant for the particular diagnosis. Especially for children who cannot read and write, this was considered not useful.

Medical language is acknowledged as difficult to understand for patients (laypeople), hence there exist projects aimed at translating medical texts (such as the electronic health record) into laypeople language more or less automatically. This rather instrumental view on language as a question of vocabulary is well established in the hospital and among medical doctors. Hence this basis for the *Sisom* project was strongly grounded in the professional context of the project.

4.2.1.3   Evidence-Based

The last of the big non-negotiable decisions in the *Sisom* project was the emphasis on evidence-based knowledge as constituting the knowledge ground that the system is built on. The symptoms to be entered into the system were not collected from patients but from medical journals. Hence the 'vocabulary' was based on how medical doctors record the symptoms of patients. The evidence-based symptoms were collected by the project leader and the psychologist; the latter had written her PhD about how children speak about their illness. Making *Sisom* rest on medical evidence obviously spoke to both doctors and the hospital administration, and was crucial for the system to be taken seriously. The list of symptoms based on literature was later subject to evaluations and modifications by child oncology experts and practitioners, as well as the participating children.

4.2.2   Decisions on How to Implement the Vision

The second kind of discussions follows from the vision, and includes how the vision was implemented. The decisions discussed below mainly reflect the values of translation and evidence-based information.

4.2.2.1   Vocabulary

The first and foremost decision to make in order to translate the *Choice* system into a 'peds-Choice' was to establish a vocabulary of symptoms of children with cancer. The vocabulary had to be based on medical evidence, hence the decision to organize the first part of the design process as a sequence of steps to achieve an evidence-based vocabulary that fit children.

The first step was to do a literature survey of reported symptoms (Vatne et al. 2010). The resulting vocabulary was evaluated by oncology experts and practitioners at the hospital, modifying and weighting the vocabulary. The decision was taken by the project leader in collaboration with the child psychologist, after the consultation with the expert practitioners. The final step of the design was a workshop with the children, categorizing, interpreting and modifying the concepts in the vocabulary. The children's categorization (e.g. that 'stomach pain' can be a symptom of nausea as well as of nightmares) confirmed that children do not distinguish between physical and cognitive in the same way as adults. The outcome of this workshop was a categorization, as well as an interpretation of everyday concepts used to describe symptoms, both kept as labels for navigation in the *Sisom* system. This decision was taken by the project leader and her core team.

4.2.2.2   Navigation mechanisms

The second aspect of translating the adult system to a child-friendly system was the interface and the navigation. The decision (by the project leader and the child psychologist) to include children who just had learnt to read and write strengthened the decision that filling out a sequence of forms was not an option. Instead the core team discussed other metaphors for navigation, ending on games as something most children are familiar with and know. The students engaged in making sketches and prototypes of games based on different metaphors, and the first workshop with the children had them try out a small selection of games and evaluate them. There was no visible decision-making after this workshop session.

However, the children later used game metaphors in their designs (e.g. shooting on your body to mark where it hurts, using a car race as a navigation metaphor) but these were discarded (see Fig. 3.10). These decisions were taken by the project leader and her core team.

The game metaphor is, however, prominent in the final *Sisom* system: the major navigation mechanism is the image of travelling to different island where different kinds of symptoms are dealt with (see Fig. 3.14). This metaphor was originally suggested by one of the informatics students (Sending 2006) and presented to the pilot group (of employees' children) before it was decided to introduce it to the children's workshops as one of the inspirational materials made by the artist.

The last decision-maker to mention here is an artist who was hired into the core team to help design a professionally looking interface. The artist's translations of the childrens' ideas (selected as important by the project leader and the core team) into professionally looking inspirational material encouraged the children to design with particular metaphors, pursuing particular kinds of expressions.

4.2.2.3   Representation

The last set of decisions that is grounded in the idea of translation is the necessity of including children in the process. The project leader decided however, that the sick children were too sick to participate in the design process, and suggested to recruit children from a nearby school to represent them.

A PD process inspired by Druin was planned with two streams of PD workshops involving two different age groups, carrying out the same activities (Druin 2002). The design decisions concerning the final user interaction as well as the vocabulary built on design ideas originating from or being confirmed and built upon in these workshops. However, the final decisions were taken by the core team after watching the video recordings of the workshops.

Healthy children can only represent severely ill children partially: they represent being children with children's logic, but representing someone severely ill requires experiences most people are fortunate to escape. Only one girl, who had experienced a severely ill relative close to her, had the empathy to imagine what that would be like. She included reasoning about her relative in evaluating some of the design moves, especially reasoning about rejecting a particular move.

4.2.3   Decisions Requiring Negotiation With the Outside World

The outside world in the form of the hospital was very present in the *Sisom* project, framing the project as well as the result. The strong emphasis on the result: a working system to be tested in use, expresses a pressure to prove useful thereby legitimizing the center and the project as such. The *Sisom* project therefore took the form of a production project of a solution.

The hardest negotiations with the outside world—the hospital—were concerned with the vision that IT can be used to enhance and support the communication between patients and health care professionals: doctors, nurses, etc. *Sisom*—and *Choice* before it—suggests including communication tools in the routines of patients and health care professionals: *Web-Choice* even suggests extending the communication between them to the home and outside of the hospital stay. These changes conflict with both legislation and current routines. Hence the project had to be defined as a research project resulting in a stand-alone system. Testing the system relied on the goodwill of the testers: the doctors and nurses as well as the patients.

This leads us to the last issue: the system is a stand-alone system not integrated in the complex IT infrastructure of the hospital. Such integration would, however, make the documentation of symptoms in the *Sisom* potentially play a role in the treatment of the patient—resulting in an even stronger voice for the patient. This is still a negotiation issue, many years after the project has ended.

4.3 Summary

Analyzing the projects made us see many different kinds of decisions influencing the design process and its result in significant ways. The big decisions were about values and concepts: the visions (Bratteteig and Wagner 2012a). These included the decision to support stakeholder participation and openness in design. They provided the normative basis for participation in the project and although participants' interpretation of them varied, they were not contested 'as such'. An example from the *Sisom* project is the decision to translate from adult to child language, which provided the basis for organizing the project. Another kind of decisions was about how to implement the vision, for example to use a game metaphor when designing the navigation mechanisms and, in the *IPCity* project, haptic tools (colored tokens) in combination with color tracking as a technical solution or to work with different representations of the site. These decisions were open to alternative solutions and some of them turned out to have implications that were not clear at the time they were taken. Yet another kind of decisions were those that required negotiations with the world outside of the project, e.g., the selection of urban projects and of participants for the workshop or the emphasis on evidence-based knowledge in the *Sisom* project. Most of the decisions were taken with no disagreement or even with no discussion, but, as we will show, some decisions involved negotiations and even conflict. In design, some of the decisions become implemented: concretized and material. Materialized decisions are intermediary or final design results. These decisions and their effects become difficult to reverse.

References

Al-Kodmany, K. (1999). Using visualization techniques for enhancing public participation in planning and design: process, implementation, and evaluation. *Landscape and Urban Planning*, *45*(1), 37–45.

Arias, E., Eden, H., Fischer, G., Gorman, A., & Scharff, E. (2000). Transcending the individual human mind—creating shared understanding through collaborative design. *ACM Transactions on Computer-Human Interaction (TOCHI)*, *7*(1), 84–113.

Bratteteig, T., & Wagner, I. (2012a). *Disentangling power and decision-making in participatory design*. Paper presented at the Proceedings of PDC 2012, Roskilde, Denmark.

Bratteteig, T., & Wagner, I. (2012b). Spaces for participatory creativity. *CoDesign*, *8*(2–3), 105–126.

Callon, M., Lascoumes, P., & Yannick, B. (2001). *Agir dans un monde incertain. Essai sur la démocratie technique*. Paris: Editions du Seuil.

Druin, A. (2002). The role of children in the design of new technology. *Behaviour and Information Technology*, *21*(1), 1–25.

Lainer, R., & Wagner, I. (1998). Offenes Planen. Erweiterung der Lösungsräume für architektonisches Entwerfen. *Architektur & BauForum*, *196*, 327–336.

Maquil, V. (2010). *The ColorTable: an interdisciplinary design process*. Vienna University of Technology, Wien, Austria.

Maquil, V., et al. (2010). IPCity. *Final prototype of urban renewal applications*. *Brussels*: European Commission.

Maquil, V., Psik, T., & Wagner, I. (2008). *The ColorTable: a design story*. Paper presented at the Proceedings of the 2nd international conference on Tangible and embedded interaction.

Maquil, V., Psik, T., Wagner, I., & Wagner, M. (2007). *Expressive Interactions Supporting Collaboration in Urban Design*. Paper presented at the Proceedings of GROUP 2007, Sanibel Island, Florida, USA.

Ruland, C. M., White, T., Stevens, M., Fanciullo, G., & Khilani, S. M. (2003). Effects of a computerized system to support shared decision making in symptom management of cancer patients: preliminary results. *Journal of the American Medical Informatics Association*, *10*(6), 573–579.

Schattschneider, E. E. (1957). Intensity, visibilit, direction and scope. *The American Political Science Review*, *51*(4), 933–942.

Sending, V. A. (2006). *En kvalitativ undersøkelse av elementer som motiverer barn til å bruke et diagnostiseringssystem*. (Master thesis), Oslo University.

Shaer, O., et al. (2004). The TAC paradigm: specifying tangible user interfaces. *Personal and Ubiquitous Computing*, *8*(5), 359–369.

Vatne, T. M., Slaugther, S., & Ruland, C. M. (2010). How children with cancer communicate and think about symptoms. *Journal of Pediatric Oncology Nursing*, *27*(1), 24–32.

Wagner, I. (2011). Building urban narratives: collaborative site-seeing and envisioning in the MR Tent. *Computer Supported Cooperative Work (CSCW)*, *21*(1), 1–42.

Chapter 5
Streams of Decisions

The notion of 'streams of decisions' reflects the fact that decisions are interrelated in different ways and that some decisions are more important than others, as they shape the space for many other decisions. In this chapter we examine how decisions are linked, with some decisions affecting other decisions in unforeseen ways. We also introduce the notion of non-decisions: choices that are made without explicitly deliberating or communicating about them.

5.1 Decision Linkages

A PD project is different from most situations the organizational literature refers to: 'move experiments' are mixed with ethnographic techniques of observation, the creation of representations, and numerous debates on a whole host of issues, some of them technical, others about values and the vision, again others about priorities, resources, and so forth. The so-called 'garbage can model' proposes to

> view a choice opportunity as a garbage can into which various kinds of problems and solutions are dumped by participants as they are generated. The mix of garbage in a single can depends on the mix of cans available, on the labels attached to the alternative cans, on what garbage is currently being produced, and on the speed with which garbage is collected and removed from the scene. (Cohen et al. 1972, p. 2)

It may be tempting to submit to the 'garbage can' model of decision-making, in particularly in highly complex projects with lots of stakeholders and a certain level of ambiguity. However, there are other ways of looking at decision-making in PD worthwhile exploring. Although different stakeholders may have hugely differing perspectives, PD uses tools and techniques that have been devised to prevent a situation where 'various kinds of problems and solutions are dumped by participants as they are generated'. We expect more 'orderly' ways of generating and handling choices.

But how do we portray the dynamics of decision-making in a PD project? This is both, a conceptual and a methodological question. In the previous chapter we have singled out certain 'design moves' as decisions. However, we do not want to suggest

T. Bratteteig, I. Wagner, *Disentangling Participation,* Computer Supported
Cooperative Work, DOI 10.1007/978-3-319-06163-4_5,
© Springer International Publishing Switzerland 2014

looking at decision-making as a series of separate decision-making episodes. Some theorists have argued that we can only determine what the choices are when looking back in a 'reflective attitude' (Schütz 1954, p. 106) or an act of 'reflection-on action' (Schön 1983, 1987). Langley et al. carry the argument further:

> First, while the concept of "decision" itself (which we take to mean commitment to action) may imply distinct, identifiable choice, in fact many decisions cannot easily be pinned down, in time or in place. [...] Third, even when a decision can be isolated, rarely can the process leading up to it. During the "long process of appraisal", to quote Dewey and Bentley (1949, p. 247), decisions typically become inextricably intertwined with other decisions. (Langley et al. 1995, p. 261)

This view on decision-making fits with our two project experiences. We may in many cases only be able in retrospect to identify a 'decision', a choice that has been made, working our way backwards, trying to reconstruct the process that led to this particular choice. We may then discover that this particular choice is 'inextricably intertwined' with a series of other choices. What Langley et al. contend is that 'research in this area would be more productive if conceived in terms of continuing and interacting streams of issues that spin off actions, *sometimes* through identifiable decisions (Langley et al. 1995, p. 270). They have identified different types of decision-linkages: sequential, precursive and lateral ones, and developed a whole taxonomy of linkages, some of which we find valuable in analyzing both projects.

The view on decision-making as 'a complex network of issues involving a whole host of linkages, more or less tightly coupled' (ibid, p. 275) fits well with our experience that a number of choices made in both projects had unforeseen implications and that some of them were paramount in the sense of defining the context for all other choices. Figure 5.1 provides an overview of decision linkages, which will be further detailed and explained in our analysis.

5.2 Handling Streams of Interrelated Issues

Looking at decisions in the two projects as streams of interrelated issues and linkages captures how some of the decisions are intertwined and affect each other, and how some decisions spur others. Interdependencies between decisions can reveal how some decisions frame processes—and other decisions—and therefore have much larger effects than what is visible on first sight.

Sequential linkages characterize decisions where one decision leads to a series of others, either smaller ones (*nesting*) or larger ones (*snowballing*) or simply the same decision *recurring*, when a problem is difficult to resolve. These types of linkages are characteristic of the sequences of 'moves' that are directed towards a design result Schön and Wiggins (Schön and Wiggins 1992) describe. We find examples of *nesting* in both projects. In *IPCity* the decision to bring MR outdoors spurred a series of decisions about the details of the tent construction and about requirements for tracking, to mention the most important. The original decision about the haptic interface also was followed by a number of smaller decisions concerning the design

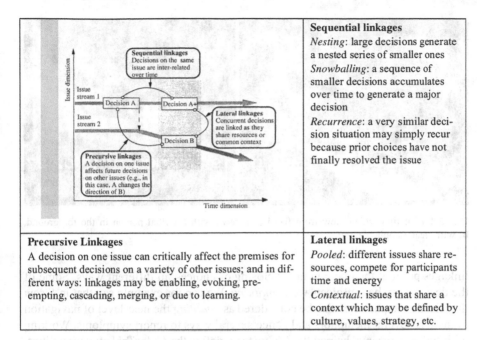

	Sequential linkages
	Nesting: large decisions generate a nested series of smaller ones
	Snowballing: a sequence of smaller decisions accumulates over time to generate a major decision
	Recurrence: a very similar decision situation may simply recur because prior choices have not finally resolved the issue
Precursive Linkages A decision on one issue can critically affect the premises for subsequent decisions on a variety of other issues; and in different ways: linkages may be enabling, evoking, preempting, cascading, merging, or due to learning.	**Lateral linkages** *Pooled*: different issues share resources, compete for participants time and energy *Contextual*: issues that share a context which may be defined by culture, values, strategy, etc.

Fig. 5.1 Types of decision linkages. (Langley et al. 1995)

of the tokens and of the interaction. In *Sisom* we see that the big decision that children with cancer are too sick to participate in the design generated a *nested* series of smaller decisions about how to best represent them in the design process. Making the island the main navigation metaphor for *Sisom* was a decision that introduced the possibility to decide on different navigation metaphors for each of the islands. *Snowballing* captures the fact that a couple of smaller decisions 'snowball' into a major one. An example from *Sisom* is when the children tried out the prototypes while in bed, saying that the game prototype looked not 'serious enough': nonetheless the decision was to keep the game-like presentation while the dinosaur-version which was also tested by the kids was dismissed. This was a major decision that built on a series of small decisions about which kinds of game-like features to incorporate in the design: while the possibility to create your own figure (avatar) to explore the islands was included, the children's racing and shooting suggestions were excluded.

Both projects demonstrated that stakeholder participation is a choice that makes *recurrent* decisions necessary. In *IPCity* the sequence of decisions that had to be taken each time a participatory workshop was planned included: the selection of sites, participants, urban issues, viewpoints for panoramas, visual content, and more. In *Sisom* selecting elements from the children's design ideas each time confronted the project team with the difficulties of giving users a say.

The *precursive* linkages observed in the projects demonstrate several ways in which a decision can affect future decisions on related other issues. *Precursive*

Fig. 5.2 Real time video view from fixed camera **a)** with a virtual person in the foreground, **b)** with 'real' people playing

linkages point at the opening up or closing of choices, in different ways. Some of the decisions in both projects were *enabling*. We can for example say that in *Sisom* the island metaphor can also be considered as *enabling* the next level of navigation to include several metaphors and hence several ways to report symptoms. Working with 'urban concepts' helped the *IPCity* team define the *ColorTable* functionalities.

Also the gift of a video camera can be considered *enabling*. One of the project partners had decided to develop a video application, the *UrbanSketcher*, which would allow participants to annotate mixed reality scenes directly 'on the projection screen'. Hence a powerful video camera in front of the *MR-Tent* came as a gift. It enabled an additional representation of the site. Another choice that opened up with the video camera was a 'mobile scouting' application, which the partner institution's virtual reality and computer graphics specialists were interested in implementing: a mobile video camera carried by a 'scout' which would widen the possibilities of 'seeing' a site from different viewpoints. The mobile scout turned into an absolute priority for the urban planner team. When it finally became available, workshop participants were delighted by both, the fixed and the mobile video view. Although lacking depth information, both views brought reality elements, such as leaves moving in the wind, people or cars passing by into the mixed reality scenes (Fig. 5.2). This was a decision that had been worthwhile to carry through practical difficulties.

In *IPCity* working with panoramas illustrates how new opportunities or problems may be *evoked* by a decision: e.g., the physical maps, the modeling of the panoramas (height and depth maps), the need for editing to make the site visible. In *Sisom* the big decision about making a PD project introduced the difficult problem of whom to involve and with it the representativity problem. The decision to use a game-like metaphor evoked some problems when the children actually drew images inspired by games they know—obviously including violence: shooting and car racing, but also some possibilities like the children using *Sisom* in an exploratory way, like a game.

Cascading linkages, when one decision 'set(s) off a series of decisions on a wide range of issues' (Langley et al. 1995, p. 274), is yet another type of *precursive* linkages. In the *IPCity* project the decision to emphasize immediacy (against simulation) spurred a range of decisions, such as for example the decision to work with panoramas as representations of a site (instead of a 3D model). It also influenced the project team's approach to working with sound (panorama sound as well as flow sounds), and shaped a range of decisions concerning interaction design. In *Sisom* the decision to make a child-friendly interface included a variety of issues, including vocabulary, interpretations, images, styles, and navigation structures.

Precursive linkages can also be seen as the effect of *learning*. 'Mutual learning' is a key concept in PD: hence we would expect many such linkages. Numerous decisions concerning the tracking algorithm and interaction design in *IPCity* were due to a learning effect through iterations of 'see-move-see'. An example of 'mutual learning' is from one of the workshops, where the participating architect redesigned 'his' bridge based on the observations and suggestions of other stakeholders. Here an earlier decision was questioned and new choices opened up due to learning. 'Lack of precision' was a concern of the urban planning team, which occasioned a number of design choices, including the modeling of the panoramas. It was due to learning from workshop participants that the urban specialists understood that 'precision' may not matter so much when the task is to create a vision for an urban site.

Interrelationships between decisions may be 'involving links between different issues being considered concurrently' (Langley et al. 1995, p. 270). *Pooled* linkages are between decisions that share resources. In *IPCity* the work on sound competed with other time-consuming work tasks, like tracking and light, about a limited set of resources in the project. In *Sisom* we can see the parallel design of several navigation metaphors (islands, the body, a tree, a house) in the beginning seen as competing for constituting the navigation metaphor.

Sometimes decisions are interrelated because 'they bathe within the same organizational context, involving the same people, the same structural design, the same strategies, and the same organizational culture and traditions' (Langley et al. 1995, p. 273). These *contextual* linkages can be seen for example in *Sisom* where the design of the icons and genre needed to fit the navigation structure, also under construction. In *IPCity* the big decisions of openness, stakeholder participation and bringing MR outdoors created such a context.

Decision-making in *IPCity* also points to a lack of linkages. So were decisions concerning the tracking mechanism made in different places and by different people. As we saw they were not well enough aligned and misunderstandings about the use situation arose. Working with sound, although well integrated conceptually and with the token and interaction design, proved to be difficult to link for workshop participants in use.

5.3   Decisions and Nondecisions

In a paper on power in community decision-making Bachrach and Baratz have introduced the notion of 'non-decisions', which they have later defended against some criticism. Nondecision-making, they argue, results from situations in which powerful actors prevent certain problems to become an issue:

> When the dominant values, the accepted rules of the game, the existing power relations among groups, and the instruments of force, singly or in combination, effectively prevent certain grievances from developing into full-fledged issues which call for decisions, it can be said that a nondecision-making situation exists. (Bachrach and Baratz 1963, p. 641)

Nondecision-making is distinct from not arriving at a decision in as it 'serves a radically different set of purposes than does decision making, and on both levels of the political process' (Bachrach and Baratz 1975, p. 902); the two levels being the formal decision-making arena and the 'covert level of politics'. Bachrach and Baratz argue that 'political consensus is commonly shaped by status-quo defenders, exercising their power resources, and operates to prevent challenges to their values and interests' (ibid, p. 901). Hence, some kinds of decisions that potentially threaten the power structures are prevented from ever appearing on the 'agenda'. Agenda control is one of many mechanisms to prevent issues from being openly discussed (Borum and Enderud 1981; Star and Strauss 1999; Strauss 1979):

- agenda control: what is discussed and who decides the themes;
- participants: who is invited in;
- scope: which solutions are possible—and hence, which problems are defined (and judged relevant) and therefore addressed;
- resources: time and people available. (Bratteteig et al. 2012, p. 130).

Reflecting on the conditions for nondecision-making Bachrach and Baratz refer to the 'mobilization of bias' as a feature of organizations that supports this covert forms of exercising power (Schattschneider 1957). 'Bias' and 'ambiguity' are phenomena that have been widely discussed within organizational theory. For example, March used the notion of ambiguity for explaining what he thinks of as 'loose coupling' between information and decision-making (March 1987). Karl Weick refers to sources of ambiguity in organizations (after McCaskey 1982), among them:

> The nature of the problem is itself in question; information (amount and reliability) is problematical; multiple, conflicting interpretations; different value orientations, political/emotional clashes; goals are unclear or multiple and conflicting; time, money or attention are lacking: contradictions and paradoxes appear; roles vague, responsibilities unclear. (Weick 1985, p. 123)

What the work of Bachrach and Baratz adds to this debate is the strategic use of bias or ambiguity in order to prevent issues to be discussed and choices to be made. Part of the criticism addressed to them had to do with the question of how to empirically identify nondecision-making. Their response to this criticism is:

> First, nondecision making ... is an act, performed either overtly or covertly, that is susceptible to observation and analysis. Second, the mobilization of bias is an effective instrument

of power and is also observable in its nature and impact; true, it is not an "event," but its existence is demonstrable both by reference to its impact upon those who wish to transform their grievances into issues and by reference to its linkage to (nondecision makers) who shape and support it. (Bachrach and Baratz 1975, p. 902)

We find nondecision-making an interesting category as it can be connected to a Foucauldian notion of power, which we will introduce in the next chapter: a form of power which is enacted through framing what is perceived in a particular situation, which may result in particular choices never moving onto the stage of a deliberation.

5.4   Nondecisions in a PD Project

When thinking about nondecisions in the context of PD it is important to remind ourselves that the 'covert exercise of power' is certainly not in the intention of the participatory designer. However, we found examples of nondecisions in both projects that are important to reflect upon.

The first example is from *IPCity*. Towards the end of the third project year the designer team discussed the possibilities of moving from a constellation of physical table and color tracking to a multi-touch version of the *ColorTable*. This discussion never moved to the decision-making stage, for a variety of reasons. First of all, the participatory designer lacked the expertise to be able to 'push' for such a decision: it was not clear how much design effort would be needed and what the advantages apart from replacing the color tracking were. Secondly, the *ColorTable* in its present shape occupied the centre of the stage: would such a decision require abandoning the strong focus on materials and haptic engagement?

We see this as a case of ambiguity: the design option of a multi-touch interface was discussed within the designer team but not clarified sufficiently to encourage a decision. The bias that surrounded the multi-touch solution also reveals a reluctance to give up things of value: the designer team was simply in love with the complex and attractive haptic interface and did not want to give up all the effort that had gone into developing it. This blurred the visibility of others solutions and the new options these may offer. Important to add that the multi-touch solution was never brought to the attention of the urban team. However, two members of the designer team used a visit to Canterbury University (NZ) as an occasion for developing a first prototype of a multi-touch solution and successfully tested it in the context of a small workshop (Fig. 5.3). This initiative came too late to be taken up in the project.

Also in the *Sisom* project some examples of nondecisions were experienced, both big and small. The decision to utilize the metaphor of a game for navigation also implies giving up the idea that the user goes through a predetermined sequence of forms or set of symptoms like in the adult *Choice* system. To deviate from the comprehensive reporting of all relevant symptoms in *Sisom* can be considered a nondecision, as it was not discussed as such but simply resulted from the choice of the island metaphor. It had important consequences, as it leaves a larger responsibility to the health care professional who has to ensure that all relevant symptoms will

Fig. 5.3 The multi-touch version of the *ColorTable*

be addressed. The surprising fact that many of the children actually explore every island is no guarantee that all relevant issues are noticed and addressed. Even if the *Sisom* system therefore is less comprehensive than the adult version, its use by sick children showed that more symptoms than before are covered. Another nondecision is the possibility for the *Sisom* system to produce a documentation of the children's view of their symptoms, adding to the already existing documentation in the patient record. This was not openly discussed in the project.

A last nondecision to mention is the project leader's lack of interest in the researcher's fieldwork. However, the usage of *Sisom* expanded from being seen as a preparation for the meeting with the doctor to a system staying with the patients at all times, hence giving them the possibility to record and document symptoms whenever they want. We make the point that this nondecision seems similar to the multi-touch nondecision in *IPCity* being grounded in feeling attached to the original vision.

5.5 Summary

A close look at the two projects has helped identify some of the decisions made and how they affected other decisions. In line with other studies of design, we found that some of the most important decisions: the big decisions, were taken very early in the project, even before all relevant knowledge is known or identified. They may close off options that will never be discussed. The big decisions are about values and frame the project and many later decisions. However, also decisions concerning how to implement the value decisions framed the projects profoundly. In design, some of these decisions become implemented: concretized and material, hence difficult to reverse, as do their effects.

The notion of decision linkages has been developed as part of organization theory. The context of design is different. However, we find it valuable to look at designing as handling interrelated streams of issues; not least as it allows us understand what it is that participants actually participate in. The different types of decision linkages are useful for seeing how decisions are linked over time (*sequential* linkages); that some decisions frame and constitute the context for later decisions or even have a pervasive effect (*precursive* linkages); and that decisions may be linked because they share resources or a common context (*lateral* linkages). Some of the linkages between decisions are obviously difficult to see at the moment of a decision, and often only possible to analyze after the fact.

Making decisions are acts of power, and our exploration of decision-making in design have also shown that the power exercised in a decision can reach longer and embrace far more than the single decision when implemented during design. It also points at interdependencies that constrain the power of decision-making.

References

Bachrach, P., & Baratz, M. S. (1963). Decisions and nondecisions: An analytical framework. *The American Political Science Review, 57*(3), 632–642.

Bachrach, P., & Baratz, M. S. (1975). Power and its two faces revisited—a reply to Geofrey Debham. *The American Political Science Review, 69*(3), 900–904.

Borum, F., & Enderud, H. (1981). *Konflikter i organisationer: Belyst ved studier af edb-systemarbejde (Conflicts in organisations, illustrated by cases of computer systems design)*. Copenhagen: Nyt Nordisk Forlag Arnold Busck.

Bratteteig, T., Bødker, K., Dittrich, Y., Mogensen, P. H., & Simonsen, J. (2012). Methods: organising principles and general guidelines for participatory design projects. In J. Simonsen & T. Robertson (Eds.), *Routledge international handbook of participatory design* (pp. 177–144). London: Routledge.

Cohen, M. D., March, J. G., & Olsen, J. P. (1972). A garbage can model of organizational choice. *Administrative Science Quarterly, 17*(1), 1–25.

Langley, A., Mintzberg, H., Pitcher, P., Posada, E., & Saint-Macary, J. (1995). Opening up decision-making. *Organization Science, 6*(3), 260–279.

March, J. G. (1987). Ambiguity and accounting: The elusive link between information and decision-making. *Accounting, Organization, and Society, 12*(2), 153–168.

McCaskey, M. B. (1982). *The executive challenge: Managing change and ambiguity*. Marshfield: Pitman.

Schattschneider, E. E. (1957). Intensity, visibility, direction and scope. *The American Political Science Review, 51*(4), 933–942.

Schön, D. A. (1983). *The reflective practitioner*. San Francisco: Harper Collins.

Schön, D. A. (1987). *Educating the reflective practitioner*. San Francisco: Jossey-Bass.

Schön, D. A., & Wiggins, G. (1992). Kinds of seeing and their function in designing. *Design Studies, 13*, 135–156.

Schütz, A. (1954). Concept and theory formation in the social sciences. *The Journal of Philosophy, 51*(9), 257–273.

Star, S. L., & Strauss, A. (1999). Layers of silence, arenas of voice: The ecology of visible and invisible work. *Computer Supported Cooperative Work, 8*(1/2), 9–30.

Strauss, A. (1979). *Negotiations: Varieties, contexts, processes, and social order*. San Francisco: Jossey-Bass.

Weick, K. E. (1985). Sources of order in underorganized systems: Themes in recent organizational theory. In Y. S. Lincoln (Ed.), *Organizational theory and inquiry* (pp. 106–136). Beverly Hills: Sage.

Chapter 6
Power, Influence, Trust and Loyalty

Power is a key concept within social and political theory. Without being able to give justice to such a complex concept and its history, we want to first point to some of its most salient roots to then highlight aspects of the concept of power that have been developed in different theoretical traditions and are relevant for our analysis.

Of enormous influence was and still is the definition of power by Max Weber (1978) and the distinction between power and domination he made. Power is the chance to exert one's own will within a social relationship, even against resistance (Dahl 1957). Domination is an institutionalized form of power; it is based on particular constellations of economic or political interests and/or authority; and it presupposes a certain willingness to obey, which is grounded in the belief that there is a 'legitimate order'. Although Weber himself has not been consistent in his use of the word 'legitimate', it indicates that something is done 'in the right way'. As specified in 'Wirtschaft und Gesellschaft' this 'rightness' can be based in tradition, in (religious) belief, or in the legal order. Legitimacy is a form of social approval that stabilizes power relations, different from the power relations in a feudal society. Max Weber has not examined why individuals come to accept the 'legitimate order'. In his theory of bureaucracy he focuses on how specific structural characteristics efficiently discipline individual action. There was a strong morality of his position, Stokes and Clegg argue:

> Weber was concerned to mount a moral case in favour of rational-legal bureaucracy. This was primarily constituted in terms of liberal ideals of governance; hence, the characterization of bureaucracy as rule without regard for persons premised on democratic ideals against blandishments of power and privilege. It was both a moral and abstractedly ideal empirical description, which, for much of the 20th century, stood as a proximate model of what public sector responsibility was founded upon. (Stokes and Clegg 1996, p. 228)

Karl Marx formulated a theory of power (and distribution) to which work as the social process of shaping and transforming the material and social worlds, is central; and which looks at capital as social power: it provides 'the power to appropriate the products of society and to subjugate the labor of others by means of such appropriation' (Marx and Engels 1848). Social theory following a Marxian tradition has subsequently formulated issues of power in terms of a 'control/resistance dualism': management (capital) controls labor—labor exercises different forms of resistance.

T. Bratteteig, I. Wagner, *Disentangling Participation,* Computer Supported
Cooperative Work, DOI 10.1007/978-3-319-06163-4_6,
© Springer International Publishing Switzerland 2014

Building on the importance of economic capital for social systems Pierre Bourdieu emphasizes symbolic power as the dominating factor in constituting as well as reproducing hierarchies of power in society (Bourdieu 1979). Formalized (hierarchical) and economic (capital) power is both necessary for maintaining dominance, but not sufficient to explain persisting hierarchies of power: also the social capital is important. Social position influence people's language (accent, grammar, spelling and style) and their cultural taste. Such cultural capital is a major element in social mobility and in maintaining social classes.

The adoption of psychoanalytical theory has widened this discourse and also added a new dimension to it. Norbert Elias builds his 'Theory of the civilization process' on Weber's sociology of domination (Elias 1976), focusing on the psychological and motivational foundations of domination. He offers a historical analysis of how the emerging control and surveillance structures of modern societies have contributed to a corresponding psychic apparatus of control. On the basis of detailed historical material he shows how prohibitions and sanctions became gradually interiorized into efficient forms of self-control. Elias criticized Freud for not taking into account that what he described as the seemingly unchangeable characteristics of the psychic apparatus are in fact subject to extraordinary changes. He used the term 'figuration' to delineate specific interdependencies of social standards and their 'imprints' in the inner life of individuals, without, however, looking closer into how social structures become 'translated' into psychic dispositions (Lemke 2001).

Feminist research has had and still has an enormous influence on how issues of power are addressed, both theoretically and empirically, and there is a vast corpus of literature on power as the organization of gender inequalities. Joan Acker introduced the term 'gendered processes' into organizational theory: it 'means that advantage and disadvantage, exploitation and control, action and emotion, meaning and identity, are patterned through and in terms of a distinction between male and female, masculine and feminine' (Acker 1992, p. 149).

When looking at how the concept of power is used today we see an enormous variety, which sometimes borders confusion. Michel Crozier starts his 1973 essay 'The problem of power' pointing at the difficulties of arriving at a concept of power:

> The concept of power is, in fact, extremely difficult to deal with. It is too vague and too ambiguous, and it too easily explains too many problems. Worse, it is difficult to clarify it, since its imprecision, and the contradictions it raises, stem not from the uncertainty of the word "power", but from the ambiguity of the facts of power themselves. (Crozier 1973, p. 213)

Similarly, Hanna Pitkin in her book 'Wittgenstein and justice' (Pitkin 1973) points to power as 'an extremely troubling' concept. Then the question is how to address these power issues: on which aspects of 'an extremely troubling' concept to build our analysis. Our approach to understanding power in PD is informed by two strands of theory: theories of power in organizations, which are in themselves varied; and notions of power based on the writings of Foucault. We will look more deeply into these different approaches to conceptualizing power, asking in how far they can help us understand the phenomena we observed in the two projects.

6.1 Power in Organizations

In the tradition of Wittgenstein Pitkin suggests to not look into what power is but into how the word 'power' is used. As already mentioned, she makes a distinction between 'power over' and 'power to' (see the French word 'pouvoir'), stressing that these two uses of the word 'power' express rather different phenomena. 'Power over' another person ('by his getting the other to do something, but also by his doing something to the other') is a relational concept; 'power to' is not defined as relational. It denotes 'capacity, potential, ability, or wherewithal' (ibid, p. 276). 'Power to' is also at the heart of Kanter's distinction between productive and oppressive power. Productive power in organizations rests on 'open channels to supplies, support, and information'. In contrast, powerlessness can 'corrupt' and often results in people 'holding others back and punishing with whatever threats they can muster' (Kanter 1979, p. 65 and 67).

Pitkin also insists on the distinction between 'power' and 'influence, which are often treated as (almost) the same (notably by Robert Dahl). Quoting Hannah Arendt, she points to the need to take account of 'human affairs [...] in their authentic diversity' (Pitkin 1973, p. 277). The trouble is, she says that 'power' and 'influence' are not mutually exclusive categories of phenomena. Unlike apples and pears they do not have neat boundaries but they are also 'not strictly comparable. They are of different kinds, or move in different dimensions' (ibid, p. 279).

German sociologist (Zündorf 1986) takes up these differences, distinguishing between four regulatory mechanisms in organizations: power (in the sense of 'power over'), influence, trust, and what he calls 'understanding' ('Verständigung'). Although these categories are of different kinds, mixing processes with results, they point at important phenomena that should not all be subsumed under the concept of power. In contrast to power, influence is based on reputation and persuasiveness; it is realized through giving explanations and trying to convince. To exert influence means to get others agree with one's claims, opinions or intentions:

> While power represents an intervention in the action space of others, influence has to begin with one's interaction partners' own dispositions to act: how they develop opinions and take decisions and not—as in the case of power—with pushing through what already has been decided. (Zündorf 1986, p. 38)

Zündorf describes two kinds of influence. Using one's knowledge and ability to solve problems for one's own advantage is a strategic, success-oriented form of influence. It is close to using power. Influence can also be oriented towards achieving consensus. Then it operates on the basis of arguments, trying to convince others. This form of influence is close to what Zündorf calls 'understanding', which is oriented towards an open dialogue. The concept goes back to Habermas, who in 'Theory of communicative action' has argued that 'a consent looses its quality of shared conviction as soon as the concerned person realizes that it results from external influence of the other on him' (Habermas 1981, p. 574). Zündorf defines 'understanding' as the 'opposite pole of power'. Between these two poles are different modes of influence. With Hannah Pitkin we think that these distinctions are important:

> The ordinary-language philosopher is interested in the borderlines of concepts, in fine distinctions, in the minutiae of our language [...] For example, the dictionary will define (one sense of) "authority" as "The power to influence action, opinion or belief." But the ordinary-language philosopher will be concerned with the way "authority" differs from "power" or "influence". (Pitkin 1973, p. 9)

The literature on decision-making in organisations introduces two additional concepts: trust and loyalty. Trust includes the feeling that one can somehow rely upon others—it is the 'confident expectation of the benign intention' of others (Dunn 1990, p. 74). Trust is required in situations where the outcome of a decision is open; it implies a certain amount of risk. In modern society trust often involves the delegating of power to people who have the expertise to solve a problem competently (or to a system that appears 'reliable': Giddens 1991). A concept that is related to trust (and confidence) but has not been discussed much within sociology is loyalty. Barbelet subsumes all three concepts under 'social emotions', saying that 'confidence is the affective basis of action and agency; trust, of cooperation; and loyalty, of organization' (Barbalet 1996, p. 75). Loyalty is for Barbalet 'the feeling of confidence that trust between others [...] can be maintained in the long run and therefore restored in the future if absent at any given time' (ibid, p. 80). Trust may be temporarily undermined. He further elaborates this idea:

> It is precisely the feeling of loyalty which maintains relationships when they might otherwise collapse, and which assumes, implicitly or explicitly, that irrespective of present circumstances, the thing to which one is loyal will be viable in the future. (ibid, p. 80, 79)

We think that both concepts, trust and loyalty, are relevant to understanding issues of power in PD. In analysing a PD project Pedersen has argued that participants often '... have dual loyalties and are double agents. ... [They] may find themselves in a precarious situation in balancing between the demands of their constituency and those of their collaborators' (Pedersen 2007, p. 123, 126).

In his book 'Negotiations' Anselm Strauss has added to this debate without, however, focusing on the concept of power as such. He considers all social orders as negotiated orders in some sense, even though negotiation may be found in combination with other processes—'notably coercion, manipulation, persuasion and the like' (Strauss 1979, p. 235)—words that express various strategies of what Pitkin calls 'power over':

> Negotiation is not merely one specific human activity or process, of importance primarily because it appears in particular relationships (diplomacy, labor relations, business transactions, and so on), but is of such major importance in human affairs that its study brings us to the heart of studying social orders. [...] A given social order, even the most repressive, would be inconceivable without some forms of negotiation. (ibid)

Strauss stresses that there are no 'ultimate limits' to negotiation, although the scope of what is negotiated may vary fundamentally, from small, short-term to large-scale issues. However, it should be noted that negotiation is not just *any* process but a particular arrangement that requires that the participating parties exchange views and mutually accommodate these views, at least to a certain extent. To draw on Zündorf's distinction: it is a process that may involve power, influence, trust, and loyalty. Also for Michel Crozier negotiation forms an important aspect of social relationships. In his essay on 'The problem of power' he, in a Weberian sense, distinguishes

> between the problem of authority—any form of power recognized as legitimate by law, custom, or a sufficient consensus of those subject to it—and the problem of power in general—that is, all relationships between men characterized by the phenomena of dependence, manipulation, or exploitation. (Crozier 1973, p. 214)

Similar to Kanter, Crozier defines power as not just oppressive but as productive, a 'positive expression' of the social control that is vital to the success of any collective effort. In his view a major organizational change has been from the 'rule of morality' (in which issues of legitimacy in the sense of 'good' and 'bad' are in the foreground) to a 'rule of negotiation', where power resides in the ability to arrive at a decision under conditions of ambiguity or uncertainty—in the sense of 'power to'. This suggests that 'power to' also is relational.

> In negotiating with the organization, a player's power ultimately depends on the control he has over a source of uncertainty that affects the pursuit of the organization's aims, and on the importance of this source as compared with other relevant sources. In negotiating with another player, his power depends on the control he can exercise over a source of uncertainty affecting this other player's behavior within the context of the rules imposed by the organization. (Crozier 1973, p. 220)

The notion of 'power play' or 'power rituals' has been taken up and elaborated by several analysts of organizations. Hardy and Glegg in 'Some dare call it power' suggest

> … to treat all forms of power play, including its theorising, as moves in games that enrol, translate and treat others in various ways, in various situated moralities, according to various codes of honour and dishonour which constitute, maintain, reproduce and resist various forms and practices of power under their rubric. There is no reason to think that all games will necessarily share one set of rules, or be capable of being generated from the same deep and underlying rule set. Power requires understanding in its diversity even as it resists explanation in terms of a singular theory. (Hardy and Clegg 1996, p. 636)

For both, Crozier and Hardy and Clegg, power requires organization; the organization (or context) in which people act and interact imposes particular 'rules of the game'—rules in the sense of 'correct conduct'. Hence, there is the power to define the 'rules of the game', which in turn poses limits to how power is practiced. As Schmidt reminds us, rule following (in a Wittgensteinian sense) also includes the ability of actors to explain, justify, sanction, reprimand, etc. actions with reference to rules, and often also the ability to teach rules, formulate rules, debate rules, etc.' (Schmidt 2011, p 372). Power is much about defining, knowing how to interpret, and modifying rules of conduct. Karl Weick has argued that uncertainty or ambiguity can be a resource to those who have the power to 'take advantage of some of the unique opportunities for change that occur when ambiguity increases' (Weick 1985, p. 126).

Coming back to Crozier, it is important to note that 'power as practice' is shaped and constrained by institutionalized aspects of power that are not so easily amenable to negotiation: 'Each power relationship is shaped by a whole series of "structural" constraints that condition the rules of the game, and it therefore expresses, at a secondary level, the logic of the institutions or structures' (Crozier 1973, p. 214). He also emphasizes that when negotiation threatens to undermine the organized system it is suppressed. Hence, 'those in power' may have a strong interest in curtailing the space for negotiation. Also Strauss underlined that 'larger structural considerations need to be explicitly linked with microscopic analyses of negotiation processes' (Strauss 1979, p. 235). Defending his notion of 'negotiated order' against the criticism of neglecting power structures he quotes a summary of the perspective formulated by Day and Day (1977):

> In the case of negotiated order theory, the individuals in organizations play an active, self-conscious role in the shaping of the social order. Their day-to-day interactions, agreements, temporary refusals, and changing definitions of the situations at hand are of paramount importance. Closely correlated is the perspective's view of social reality... the negotiated order theory downplays the notions of organizations as fixed, rather rigid systems which are highly constrained by strict rules, regulations, goals, and hierarchical chains of command. [...] Similarly, power is not viewed in an absolute sense but rather in its relationship to other factors which create coalitions and partnerships varying with time and circumstances.... ((Day and Day 1977) quoted in (Strauss 1979, p. 260))

It is this last point that draws attention to a problematic aspect of negotiated-order theory. Organizations need not be 'rigid systems' but may nevertheless be governed by some strict rules in the form of contractual relationships and a pronounced division of labor, both of which regulate access to knowledge, as well as economic and technical resources, limiting the power to enter negotiations and have one's voice heard. Although having been negotiated at some point, these institutionalized forms of power are not negotiable in the here-and-now of people's work situation. Morgan has compiled a long list of sources of power in organizations, which also includes structural elements: authority; control of scarce resources; use of organizational structures, rules, and regulations; control of decisions processes; control of boundaries; and so forth. Also the participatory context of a project may be bounded by structural elements that limit the possibilities for joint decision-making by, for example, restricting access to resources or commending particular ways of working (Morgan 1986).

6.2   How much and What Kinds of Power?

The sharing of power in PD is a complex interplay of mechanisms, in which different resources and multiple loyalties come to work together, and where structural arrangements limit what is negotiable and actually negotiated.

6.2.1   The Influence of Structural Arrangements

We have to keep in mind that a PD project is different from an organization in many respects. Projects in general are characterized by less formal structures and more flexibility than more long-lasting forms of organizing work (e.g., Manning and Sydow 2011; Whitley 2006). However, they may have to operate in a highly structured environment that imposes particular 'rules' and surely they have to define their own ways of operating. What do we think of as structural arrangements in both projects?

Both projects started out as 'technology projects'. The decision that computers are part of the solution had already been taken when writing the proposal. *IPCity* responded to a EU-Call on 'Presence and interaction in mixed reality'; *Sisom* built on *Choice*, a previous successful application for adults.

IPCity was a large research project with a common frame that had been defined in the form of a detailed work program. This work program was part of a contract with the European Commission, with elements that were open to interpretation and negotiation. Apart from this, the leader of the consortium had developed a project handbook that was 'brimming' with rules for decision-making. Some of these rules, in particular those concerning who was to be admitted to particular types of meetings and had the right to vote, were contested from time to time and also overridden. From the beginning, there were many dependencies to account for: the work of several geographically distributed partners had to be coordinated; moreover, the plan of conducting participatory urban planning workshops required coordination with local projects and local authorities in France, which imposed some of their 'rules' on the project; and, ultimately, all four 'showcases' were supposed to produce a common set of 'results'.

The urban planning showcase was directed by the participatory designer. She had been part of defining the vision for the project, inviting her team into making this vision concrete and pushing for novel solutions. She had the 'last word' with respect to the allocation of resources: sure, consulting with all team members about priorities to be set and 'defending' budgetary decisions in negotiations with the *IPCity* consortium as well as the external project officer and reviewers. For example, working with panoramas required substantial resources allocated by the project leader; so did sound.

Most importantly, the project leader had decided on the skill composition of the team. Hiring a product designer, a visual artist and a musician in addition to two computer scientists meant that their skills and visions were valued and this strengthened the artistic and the design aspects of the project. Most issues were open to negotiation but some, such as the vision or specific 'requirements' were not. All team members were free and even expected to bring in their ideas and had much space for developing them. This was supported by the fact that the design process had been planned as open and iterative.

Sisom was a much smaller project with less formal rules and less dependencies. The process was much less open than the one in *IPCity*: it followed a structured model of three phases with the intent to generate a product. This introduced a particular 'logic' that did not endorse a more explorative style of working: features of the design that could not be incorporated in the product idea were not considered useful, hence discarded. Moreover, the new product had to fit into the existing sociotechnical infrastructure of the hospital. This worked as an even stronger constraint.

All the power was with the project leader who, however, had to comply with the rules of the hospital and its medical system. The children's *Choice* system had to fit into the work practices at the children's cancer ward, which were not questioned at all. It also had to comply with the standards of evidence-based medicine. The hospital research centre that employed the project leader did not impose particular and additional rules on the project, except its high interest in producing academic publications.

Also in *Sisom* the project leader selected her collaborators in the project. She looked for designer skills that were not present in the centre's IT group, among them a flash developer and a graphic designer. The psychologists she selected corresponded with what she thought the project was about: understanding children's vocabulary.

6.2.2 The 'power players'

Our next step is to look more closely at the different 'players' in the projects to see which strategies they employed for settling issues (presented in Chap. 3).

The *participatory designer* in *IPCity* took the lead in the decisions on values and concepts, which were based on long-term research interests and a strong vision. As a project leader and primary researcher she used authority, grounded in her research experience and her knowledge of the practice of urban planning. While her main strategy concerning decision-making was a mixture of influence oriented towards persuasion and creating mutual understanding, she also used power by eliminating some choices, e.g., insisting on 'immediacy' and ruling out 'simulation'. Her loyalties were divided between the designer team she was supervising, the urban planner team and her research commitments, hence the communities that represent them. Perhaps the strongest of these commitments was supporting and improving the capacity of lay stakeholders to participate.

The *designer team* in *IPCity* was responsible for the technologies, TUI and interaction design, the design of content, and the production of the panoramas. The technical design decisions regarding the use and further development of colour tracking or the ways to 'model' the panoramas were based on a mixture of influence and trust. This reflected the fact that neither the participatory designer nor the urban team was able to seriously contest decisions requiring specialized technical expertise; they could only challenge the outcomes of these decisions. TUI and interaction design, as well as the design of content were less technical, hence much more debatable and debated; here different kinds of expertise (product design, artistic, technical) met and the decision-making aimed at arriving at a mutual understanding.

The *urban planner-users* in *IPCity* not only accepted and supported the decisions based on values and concepts. They also took normative decisions concerning the representation of urban issues, leaning on the 'representational tradition' within architecture, which led to some uncontested decisions (the panoramas) but also to considerable conflicts (the editing of content). They also were in charge of negotiations with the outside world. Here they operated on the basis of influence, in both strategic and consensus-oriented ways, and the rest of the team had to trust their local knowledge and negotiation skills.

The power of *workshop participants* in *IPCity* was indirect, mainly exercised through how they used the *ColorTable*. They changed the designers' views of what they had designed, bringing imperfections but also strengths to the fore, in multiple ways. Workshop participants had to accept the frame for participation, which, however, had been deliberately made open for them in the sense that they could freely choose the urban issues they wanted to address and construct their vision. They also made choices, concerning the content that had been prepared, sometimes insisting on creating their own content (supported by a 'sketching' application). As they were short-time visitors to the project, they would keep their original loyalties, bringing in their perspectives and temporarily aligning them with those of the other partici- pants in the workshop.

The experts among the workshop participants acted in very different ways. In both of the workshops in Cergy-Pontoise the architect-planners perfectly blended into the team, which mainly consisted of 'normal' citizens, such as residents, a policeman, representatives of local commerce, and so forth. One of the participat- ing architects enthusiastically pointed out that the *ColorTable* acts as a mediator: participants did not discuss in a confrontational way but by means of gesturing, set- ting interventions, commenting, and modifying. The main alignment mechanisms at play were influence (much in the sense of persuading the other participants) and seeking mutual understanding. In contrast to this, the two architects participating in one of the two Oslo workshops dominated and framed the discussion to be very practical, fact-based and oriented towards solving problems. They took advantage of their expert position (Bratteteig and Wagner 2012b).

The power of the '*outside world*' of urban projects and local authorities in- fluenced the selection of sites and contributed to the framing of the participatory workshops. We have described that the selection of workshop participants became a 'political' issue.

In *IPCity* the fact that four external reviewers evaluated the project results at the end of each project year cannot be neglected. They, equipped with the author- ity of the funding agency, had the power to reject results, eventually even stop the funding, or enforce some redirection of the project, which they did at several oc- casions. The review meetings were, though amiable, characterized by numerous conflicts. Most of these conflicts had to do with the fact that reviewers represented disciplines, research orientations and understandings that were rather different from the vision of the project. Also, they lacked some of the expertise to judge some of the highly technical parts of the work. Although they in the end came to appreci- ate the team's work, much unplanned effort went into research tasks, the reviewers added to the agenda: such as for example a quantitative analysis of video material produced in the participatory workshops, and into 'justifying' the approach. Power on the side of reviewers met attempts at exercising strategic influence on the side of the project consortium, in which the participatory designer had a strong voice. However, she also fell back on her team to explicate and defend technical choices she would not have been able to present.

The *project leader* of the *Sisom* project was not participatory in the same way as the participatory designer in *IPCity*. She 'owned' the project, which she described as her 'dream project'. She defined the vision for the project and controlled all decisions. She used the authority of the medical system to establish an evidence-based approach as a 'must'. Her main loyalty was to the hospital staff and the children with cancer, whose treatment she hoped to be able to improve. Although she provided some space for ethnographic fieldwork, she did not recognize it as a valid approach to understanding how children talk about their symptoms. In fact, she did not open the project beyond the two design tasks she had defined. The participatory designer in the project, although originally invited to contribute, had a rather limited role.

In *Sisom* the *designer team* responsible for the *Sisom* children's version of *Choice* consisted of the centre's internal programmers, who had delivered the *Choice* system for adults and the web version of it; as well as MSc students from the University of Oslo who designed different prototypes. All of them were dependent on the approval of the project leader, hence had rather little space to exert influence. The psychologist designing the children's vocabulary cooperated with the project leader in the context of writing her PhD—also a power relationship.

The *medical and nursing staff* were included less as users of the *Sisom* system than as advisers, as well as testers of the vocabulary. Their power derived from their expert knowledge and the authority this entails. The children's role was to 'represent' how kids talk about symptoms and to develop the graphics and navigation they liked most. Although their tasks were limited, they were free in how they approached them. Much like in *IPCity* their influence was indirect. In fact, the project team did not engage in debates with them during the workshops but facilitated the design process by questions and suggestions that encouraged the children to take certain directions. The decisions were taken afterwards by the project leader, after having looked at, analysed and discussed the video material.

6.2.3   Ways of Aligning Work and Different Positions

As we have shown, power was not the only mechanism regulating decision-making. Acting within a participatory framework and doing research, requires argumentation and, ideally, participants strive for *mutual understanding*. But this is not always possible. In *IPCity* the participatory designer invested much effort in communicating the vision for the project, the acceptance of which was due to the recognition of her expertise and experience. It built on a contract, which defined the conditions for cooperation in the project. It is important to note, however, that the vision was open to the project team's interpreting and imagining. But different interpretations also created conflicts: over issues of representation but also over the value of the participation of lay people.

The conflicting positions of the participatory designer and her team on the one side, the urban planning team on the other side reemerged with each participatory workshop: with the designer team bringing a new version of the *ColorTable*, including the edited panoramas and content and the urban planner team voicing criticism and at some points even rejecting the solution. This experience reflects what Björgvinsson et al. discuss as 'agonistic PD', which is about aligning 'participants around a shared, though problematic or even controversial object of design (Björgvinsson et al. 2012, p. 109). 'Agonism', a concept that goes back to Chantal Mouffe, expresses forms of debate and confrontation that allow for 'constructive controversies between 'adversaries'. [...] These activities are full of passion, imagination and engagement' (ibid, p. 109).

Some choices in the *Sisom* project were based on creating mutual understanding. In fact, the 'adults' in the project listened carefully to the children's way of talking about symptoms and to their visual ideas. One interesting observation here is that the project members liked the idea of 'islands', because it would motivate children to behave like explorers, hopping from island to island, thereby covering the full range of possible symptoms. However, the project leader did not understand how good the island idea was but she accepted it when everyone could see how the children picked it up. An example of understanding that came late in the project is the prototyping session where the school children tried the prototype while in bed: their evaluation of the prototype suddenly became more serious, as if the situation of 'being in bed' nurtured the children's imagination about how a sick child would react.

Influence can be consensus-oriented, but it often has a strategic element and uses persuasion. This kind of influence had a certain role in the *Sisom* project. For example, the artist's task was to pick up some of the elements the children had created, make them look more professional and finished, using her professional skills and give them back to them in the next session. The persuasion was in making a selected design element appeal to the children so that they would continue working with these ideas and feel even more attracted to particular solutions.

Influence had a large part in how working with sound was argued for in *IPCity*. Sound as a highly relevant aspect of an urban planning context came to occupy a special place for debate in the project. The project leader and the urban specialist used influence (in a strategic sense) in their negotiations with reviewers and the external funding agency so as to be able to maintain this shared research commitment. But sound and the particular approach to integrating it with the mixed reality scenes turned out to be difficult to work with. It conflicted with the idea of precision, which had shaped the expectations of some of the urban specialists; and workshop participants had difficulties in relating to the possibilities of working with sound with the same ease as they manipulated the visual content. 'Sound' had to be defended and much effort was required to attract the attention of workshop participants to using it. The use of sound brought up more issues than could be resolved within the project. Here the loyalty of the project team was mainly to the vision and the connected research agenda. We see the same loyalty play out in the *Sisom* project.

Strategic and achievement-oriented influence was of importance in the negotiations with the outside world. Driving these decisions also needed some persuasion, based on the research vision. Project owners and local authorities had to be convinced that they could learn something from the participatory workshops: about participation as a method, about the power of participatory tools, but also from participants' vision for the future of the site. It was in negotiating and preparing for the workshops where the expertise and the connections of the urban planners most directly met the reality of decision-making in urban contexts.

Influence as a regulating mechanism is very common in decisions requiring highly specialized, mostly technical expertise. We will discuss in the next section how different types of expert knowledge were handled in both projects. An important observation here is that in particular in the technical decisions, influence (of the technical team) was coupled with trust (by all others). An example is the design decision in *IPCity* to use colour tracking. Once the main weakness (the sensitivity to changing light conditions) became obvious it could only survive since project participants decided to trust the technical team. They witnessed the problems of the technical solution without being able to contribute, assuming that a satisfactory solution would be found.

This example also illustrates the workings of loyalty. The decision to use colour tracking was taken by the designer team, but the algorithm was developed by a project partner. While the latter was interested in a highly sophisticated technical solution, the designer team needed a solution that worked in use, under the conditions of varying lighting conditions. We see different loyalties on the side of the developers: to the solution itself versus to how the solution would enable users to work smoothly.

Loyalty was also an issue for the urban planner team. It took them a long time to shift some of their loyalty from their own professional community to the project. Their 'double loyalties' became visible in their need for peer recognition and the conflicts this created (the instability of the prototypes, 'things being imperfect'); and the time it took them to accept and 'defend' the *ColorTable*.

In *Sisom* the decision to not enrol children with cancer also reflects loyalty: to the kids whose condition was respected. However, it was also based on practicability, as sick children would not be available for 6 weeks of workshops and testing. The project was also loyal to the doctors working with the children, and their emphasis on evidence-based medicine.

6.3   Power/Knowledge

It is almost a 'must' to refer to Foucault and his notion of power/knowledge when discussing about power. We have drawn much inspiration from Foucault's writings but also have some reservations, arguing for the need to examine his argumentation more closely.

6.3.1   The Ubiquity of Power

Foucault has seen himself as an intellectual provocateur that radically questions the notion of subject, identity, individuality, and knowledge. His thinking is deeply embedded in the French discourse of his time. With Lacan (1979) he shares a deep suspicion of the concept of 'subjective identity' (Rabaté 2003). Foucault's writings on power, in particular 'The subject and power' (1982), elaborate this notion of the ambiguous relationship the subject has with her/himself.

Foucault positions his particular approach to power in relation to theories that analyze relations of dominance and exploitation:

> It soon appeared to me that, while the human subject is placed in relations of production and of signification, he is equally placed in power relations which are very complex. Now, it seemed to me that economic history and theory provided a good instrument for relations of production and that linguistics and semiotics offered instruments for studying relations of signification; but for power relations we had no tools of study. We had recourse only to ways of thinking about power based on legal models, that is: What legitimates power? Or, we had recourse to ways of thinking about power based on institutional models, that is: What is the state? (Foucault 1982, p. 778)

Foucault has never specified how to think the interdependencies between power relations and relations of production and domination. In his reading power is a fundamental characteristic of social life, a feature of all practice. It is located in the 'micro-physics' of daily life, in the 'depths' of society: power is the 'capacity' of action to shape other action. Power is about interdependencies; and it is, as organizational theorists would formulate it, about agency. However, Foucault explicitly does not focus on identifiable people as exercising power. He argues that depersonalizing power is important if we want to understand the most effective forms of it. What makes power so effective are particular 'technologies' or regimes that construct knowledge, bodies and subjects. The body of the individual is

> ... directly involved in a political field: power relations have an immediate hold upon it; they invest it, mark it, train it, force it to carry out tasks, to perform ceremonies, to emit signs. (Foucault 1973, p. 27)

Power is immanent to economic processes, knowledge relations and sexual relations. It is associated with particular techniques or forms that regulate or 'discipline' our fundamental experiences. In his own work Foucault analyzed the genealogy of three of these disciplining regimes: methods of observation and measuring, ways of defining differences and 'normalizing', as well as the ways sexuality is defined and experienced.

One of the key technologies of the self is the 'panopticon' (Foucault 1979), which Foucault proposed as a metaphor for describing the internalization of the view of the 'other' to produce self-monitoring subjects that are disciplined by the other's gaze. The other is the 'confession' seen as a set of 'technologies':

> Since Freud, it could be argued that the secular form of confession has been 'scientised' through new techniques of normalisation and individualisation that include clinical codifications, personal examinations, case-study techniques, the general documentation and collection of personal data, the proliferation of interpretive schemas and the development of a whole host of therapeutic techniques for 'normalisation'. In turn, these 'oblige' us to be free, as self-inspection and new forms of self-regulation replace the confessional. (Besley 2005, p. 85)

The notion of quasi 'autonomous' technologies that people apply to themselves and to others can be considered the core of Foucault's analysis of power. According to him these technologies have shaped the development of the human sciences, into which they have been transposed and inserted and where they are used 'without renunciation of the self but to constitute, positively, a new self. To use these techniques without renouncing oneself constitutes a decisive break' (Foucault 1988, p. 49). Modern organizations have perfectionized power, as they entice the individual to contribute productively, to participate, to provide insight into his/her inner self of motivations, anxieties and hopes, thereby enabling the total control of behavior and a most efficient mobilization of resources.

Foucault himself stressed that he was not up to formulating a theory of power. He was interested in understanding how the subject is constituted through techniques of self-disciplining. When speaking about 'technologies of the self' Foucault adopted a concept that normally is used with reference to machines of all kinds: 'Technology is traditionally and usefully defined as rationalized or systematic knowledge of the useful "arts" or techniques' (Schmidt 2011, p. 267). In fact, Foucault talks about bodies of knowledge that have developed as a result of systematic rationalization. It remains unclear, however, what exactly Foucault means by 'rationalization'. Max Weber defined it with reference to the systematization of ideas: it is the key process, which gives ideas the capacity to influence social action. In modern science it means knowing why things work in a certain way. For Foucault 'rationalization' seems to be inevitably tied to normativity, hence power.

Highly controversial is Foucault's notion of the subject, which in turn is connected to the question of resistance: when power creates subjects that accept or internalize their position, how can they critically distance themselves from the regimes that define their very being? Judith Butler has reformulated this position:

> But if, following Foucault, we understand power as forming the subject as well, as providing the very condition of its existence and the trajectory of its desire, then power is not simply what we oppose but also, in a strict sense, what we depend on for our existence and what we harbor and preserve in the beings we are. (Butler 1997)

Foucault has argued that the ubiquity of power does not preclude resistance but this resistance cannot come from a position of exteriority. Resistance(s) can only exist in the strategic field of power relations. In a paper on 'Foucauldian feminism' Cooper voices concern with the relationship of power and resistance in Foucault's work, asking:

> Conscious (as opposed to unintended) resistance, in contrast, requires subjects to recognise the exercise of power for what it is. Is resistance then the effect of 'faulty' production—power generating wants and desires it cannot meet—or the result of layers of discourses which create different and contradictory subject positions? This raises a further question: what exactly is it that power creates? In the case of femininity, is it acquiescence, agreement? Does power provide the preconditions for 'freely' given consent, or does it ensure practices that are internalised at a level too unconscious for assent to be realised? (Cooper 1994, p. 452)

Cooper argues that whether power operates in a 'progressive or reactionary way' depends on its form, the terrain in which it operates and the wider social and historical conditions. She also makes place within a Foucauldian framework for more oppositional technologies of power that 'could include new kinds of knowledge grounded in different epistemologies, alternative cultural truths, or radical democratic processes' (ibid). It is this possibility to resist the normalizing effects of disciplinary power, which Robertson refers to reflecting on possibilities 'to continually problematise and undermine the naturalness, necessity and inevitability of the specific kinds of recoding of our behaviour that the use of communication technologies asks of us' (Robertson 2006, p. 58).

Interpreters of Foucault maintain that in his later work he has conceptualized a kind of 'anarchic subject'. Notably Hekman (2010) stresses Foucault's contribution to a 'critical ontology of ourselves': he discloses the social realities that constitute ourselves, deconstructing the power of discursive norms, pointing at what 'identity options' are open to the subject. However, Foucault has never elaborated the potential of such a subject that is capable of critical reflection and of acting and seeing differently. While criticizing mentalist and essentialist notions of the subject, Foucault also opposed theories that anchor human history in practice and subjectivity (see the excellent analysis provided by Moldaschl 2003).

So, without going deeper into the various interpretations of Foucault's work, why take up his concept of power within studies that focus on people, participation and decision-making? Foucault draws our attention to what he calls 'power/knowledge', showing how all forms of knowledge are deeply enmeshed with power practices. It is through discourse (not the subjects that speak it) that topics are constructed. Discourse defines and produces the objects of our knowledge and influences how ideas are put into practice: 'Just as discourse "rules" certain ways of talking about a topic, defining an acceptable and intelligible way to talk, write, or conduct oneself, so also, by definition, it "rules out", limits and restricts other ways of talking, of conducting ourselves in relation to the topic or constructing knowledge about it' (Hall 1997, p. 44). The link between knowledge and power is precisely that the discourse about a topic governs what is sayable and even thinkable. Foucault was immensely critical about how particular discourses in the social sciences and the humanities—their ways of conceptualizing, categorizing, and measuring—acquired authority at a certain historical moment.

Moreover, readers of Foucault, including many feminists, have been attracted by the notion that power is not necessarily 'negative'. Power or the lack of it does not only result in marginalization, exclusion, non-decision or non-action. Power as 'agent' also supports and structures the field of options, decisions and practices, and forms of individuation. While this superficially reflects the distinction between 'power on' and 'power to', we should not forget that Foucault describes 'discourse as object' and 'knowledge codes' as its rules of production (Foucault 1973, p. 200). It is power that has 'agency' rather than people.

Foucault's writings had and continue to have much influence on organizational theory. Just to mention a few examples: Burrell (1988) referring to 'The archeology of knowledge' emphasizes the power of 'normalization' in organizations; Stokes and Clegg take up Foucault's notion of 'governmentality' that captures how 'the personal projects and ambitions of individual actors become meshed with, and form

alliances with, those of organization authorities and dominant organization actors
(Stokes and Clegg 2002, p. 229); Roberts uses Foucault's notion of 'visibility' to
explore 'the operation of systems of accountability in and around organizations'
(Roberts 2005).

Much use is made of Foucault's notion of 'normalisation', which stresses how
disciplining people's thinking homogenizes (the way a topic can be talked about)
while effecting 'dividing practices' that individualize:

> In a sense, the power of normalization imposes homogeneity; but it individualizes by mak-
> ing it possible to measure gaps, to determine levels, to fix specialties and to render the dif-
> ferences useful by fitting them one to another. (Foucault 1979, p. 184)

Specialization and professionalization are seen as going hand in hand with discipline, as they build upon parceling a complex, multifarious subject matter into neat,
manageable, (hierarchically or otherwise) ordered categories. In particular Bowker
and Star (1999) have elaborated on the practices of 'normalising' and, connected to
this, the importance of attending to 'residual categories'. Reflecting on the making
of categories they observe:

> One implication is that the category is a desiccated form of a complex narrative. That is,
> it is a conclusion, wrapper, or label that points back to a long, contingent story. But the
> story itself is often permanently inaccessible. [...] Often the makers of categories have
> naturalized that which they categorize, what they are categorizing, and feel further that the
> categories are so self-evident that they need no comment. [...] They do not know how to
> usefully record messy human data. Frequently, there are political reasons to obscure the
> stories behind a category. (Star and Bowker 2001, p. 273, 274).

These arguments resonate with the notion of 'power/knowledge': knowledge that
assumes power through processes of normalization (or 'naturalization') that make
contradictory practices appear 'abnormal'. Referring to Foucault, Suchman in her
discussion of speech act theory (and the 'Coordinator') addresses the power of categories as a 'training of the body's intentions as reflected in his talk' (Suchman
1994, p. 183).

6.3.2   The Power of Competing Discourses

Two of Foucault's arguments are of particular relevance for our analysis: firstly, it is
through 'discourse' that topics are constructed; secondly, the notion of 'normalising
practices'. Looking at the different expert knowledges and modes of expression in
both projects, provides answers to: how accessible were these; how powerful, how
exposed to criticism and vulnerable; and how much did they become shared?

As both, an interdisciplinary and participatory project, *IPCity* assembled several
discourses with their specific modes of expression. The participatory designer built
her interventions on her rather broad research experiences, which enabled her to
perceive and appreciate the many interrelated aspects of the project. She communicated these experiences mainly in the form of 'stories' about observations and concepts. Embedded in these stories was a strong ethical stance. The urban expertise

was about how to understand a site and its potential and how to represent an urban situation. The team expressed this expertise verbally but also visually, e.g. producing visual examples of 'urban concepts', arguing with the help of maps and other representations of a site.

In a design project 'discourse' includes the making of things. For most project participants the technical expertise that went into the design of the *ColorTable* remained largely 'in the background'. It was something that was not communicated directly but demonstrated with the help of a prototype. The others, team members as well as workshop participants, could only observe and challenge the results of a technical decision (for example saying, 'we need more precision in placing objects in a panorama'). Workshop participants communicated primarily through their material practices of 'using'. This reflects what Finken has observed, analysing the discourses of web designers. She shows how 'in performance the designers' access to privileged knowledge about the customer's needs and usability testing marginalized the users' knowledges and standpoints' (Finken 2005, p. 207).

In *Sisom* the opportunities of having different possibly conflicting 'discourses' meet were rather limited. The project was dominated by evidence-based medicine and by research-based expertise on how children talk about symptoms: 'a pain in my stomach' can have several different reasons. The experience and input of the participating children and doctors was allowed to modify this basis. As ethnographic fieldwork was not accepted as a source of understanding actual practices neither for building a vocabulary 'bottom up', the chances to open up for the design of a much broader application (as advocated by the participatory designer) remained unexploited. From the fieldwork it had become evident that the tool might be used in many different kinds of situations, for example at home as a kind of 'diary'. These potential uses of an enjoyable low-threshold communication tool were not explored.

The ability to make things furnishes with a particular kind of power. This does not mean that non-experts don't have any voice. Engineers are confronted with the expectation that the things they design work properly. Hence, there is a significant element of vulnerability in their technical expertise. In *IPCity* this was increased by the decision to have participants work with rather early prototypes that turned out to be instable. In *Sisom* the strong focus on a product that could be integrated with the existing sociotechnical infrastructure meant to minimize the potential vulnerability by strictly focusing on representations of symptoms that pleased the participating kids.

We can also see that in a design project power may be shared as long as alternative solutions are presented, discussed and a choice is made. Then power comes to reside in the person who implements the decision, making it material. A good example is the power of editing that was shared by the visual artist and the urban planners but in the end the artist, as the person who performed the editing, took the decisions on what would become visible and how. The panoramas turned out to be 'critical' to the workshops, as the ways that they were edited (by the visual artist) shaped how participants would actually see the site. Also in *Sisom* the artist played an important role. She lend the children's drawing a professional quality, thereby creating representations of key decisions concerning the interface and navigation mechanism.

This leads to an ethical argument that was debated in *IPCity*, which is to do with the power of 'normalising'. Visual representations constitute the basis for describing and debating an urban project and their 'nature' influences the outcome of negotiations (Neto 2006). They contribute to how the negotiation procedure is initiated, structure the content of discussions and regulate who is in a position to contribute. It is well known that the use of a technical vocabulary together with plans and drawings as discussion tools influences the participation of citizens and reduces the possibility of a real exchange (Söderstrom and Zepf 1998). Moreover, visual representations are not 'innocent'—they are of a strategic nature and are influenced by a certain subjectivity, mostly that of the architect/urban planner or that of the client (Estevez 2001). Architects are trained to make visible what they want to show and to conceal what they prefer to remain diffuse or opaque. The architect's visual representations have a rhetorical dimension: they are conceived to convince, to please and seduce and they adapt themselves to their interlocutor. The use of sound to enrich the visual material complicates the question. Studies on the influence of the interaction between visual and acoustic stimuli on the perception of the environment suggest that 'the interaction of a setting's visual and acoustic characteristics significantly influences evaluation of that setting' (Anderson et al. 1983, p. 539);

> and that 'the congruence or coherence between sound and image influences preferences … a change in sound-image compatibility conditions is enough to produce quiet different aesthetic and affective reactions. Visual information and acoustic information as such can reinforce or interfere with each other' (Carles et al. 1999, p. 191, 199).

This possibility of 'manipulating' participants' perception of a site can be powerful. We think it provides a good example of what Foucault writes about 'normalising'. Latour has argued that visualizations simultaneously support constructing the artifact and staging its performance and understanding by others (Latour 1986). In this case it is not only the 'categories' we use for capturing or disclosing phenomena that need critical scrutiny, but the choice of representations. As Rogan argues, things made material (touchable, visual, auditory) may communicate qualities or ideas 'in a more subtle, elegant, discreet or economical way than a natural language is capable of' (Rogan 1992, p. 109). Much communication in design focuses on creating 'persuasive artifacts' (Wagner 2000) in the expectation to convince, seduce, invite into a dialogue or possibly hide aspects that the designer does not want to make open and disputable. This reminds us of the importance of the PD principle that users should be able to speak in their own language rather than having to use a formalized description language; and that using prototypes helps users show (rather than have to tell) (Bjerknes and Bratteteig 1987).

6.4 Shades of 'power to'

Having identified different discourses and discussed the power of normalizing we need to add a word of caution. Foucault's writings alert us to be highly sensitive to the categories and conceptual schemes we use (as do Bowker and Star 1999). The distinctions on which they rest may have this power but we have to remind here that *all* our practices are normative in the sense of there are right (or wrong) ways of doing things (Schmidt 2011). In this light it seems problematic to equal power with normativity in the way Foucault does. There is a need to make distinctions: the power/knowledge that leads to committing somebody to a psychiatric ward is different from the power/knowledge that enables a team of engineers to argue for and develop a method for colour tracking. The contexts are entirely different; so are the consequences. This difference cannot be simply resolved into 'power over' versus 'power to'. Foucault has shown how power (or better: some kind of power) shapes how we think of ourselves and of many matters in the world. His discussion of the 'double-sided character of subjection/subjectivication' together with the notion that 'discourse itself is a regulative and regulated formation' (Hall 1996, p. 23) has heightened our sensitivity to the pervasiveness of (some forms of) power. If we examine all discourse about all possible topics under the assumption that it governs what is say-able and even thinkable, thereby excluding how this could be said or thought otherwise, we miss out salient aspects of power that are do with people and their agency (Robertson 2006).

This is why we think it important to look into how power is enacted in contexts where the problems to be addressed, the perspectives on these problems and ways to finding a solution are negotiated. We already discussed the role of mechanisms such as influence, trust, loyalty or the wish to create mutual understanding. Looking at power in the context of a PD project requires asking: what are the 'rules of the game' (of correct conduct); who established them; to which extent are they contested, discussed, modified, and so forth. This fits well with the notion of 'agenda control' (Borum and Enderud 1981) discussed in Chap. 5. We have seen that contractual agreements play a large role: they define objectives and outcomes, responsibilities, resources, timelines, and so forth. In PD methods and tools play a large role: there are 'right ways' of working with users, of evaluating a design in use, and so forth. How open to modifications by participants were these rules?

In *IPCity* it was not the idea of participatory workshops as such but some of the details of how to prepare and conduct them that were contested by the urban planners. They found it difficult to accept that the prototypes were so provisional and 'immature'; that participants were expected to seriously commit themselves to spending time testing them; that they needed some preparation, and so forth. Hence, the very format of participatory workshops gave rise to conflicts, including temporary refusals. It took time and 'influence' to convince the members of the urban planner team and turn them into collaborative players.

Involvement of the children in *Sisom* followed quite strictly the 'rules' that Alison Druin had formulated on the basis of her PD projects with children (Druin 2002). The kids in *Sisom* participated in the roles of user, tester, and informant. This basis for working was only contested by the participatory designer, who saw some space for opening up the process, but she got a limited role. Doing things in the right way was defined from the beginning as complying with medical evidence. However, the fact that children were involved and taken seriously made way for a truly participatory design result.

6.5 Summary

'Design crystallizes power relations' Hyysalo and Lehenkari argue in their 'Foucault-inspired power analysis' of a design project (Hyysalo and Lehenkari 2002, p. 101). Discussing power issues in PD leads to a wide range of questions. We have addressed some. Sharing power is not straightforward. The ways both projects proceeded point at the relevance of structural arrangements, which may have considerable influence on how a PD project can possibly develop. In fact, in some participatory projects much effort is spent on negotiating a contract before engaging in an organization (Simonsen and Kensing 1994). But even then constraints, such as the purpose to develop a product that fits an existing IT infrastructure, deadlines, budget restrictions or the 'rules' the world outside the project impose, may limit the possibilities to widen the design space and maintain it open. Asking 'who initiates and benefits', Vines et al. observe:

> We might assume that initiation is led by members of the project team performing a study or designing a particular system. It is often these individuals who recruit participants, lead workshops and act as a point of contact for those taking part. If we continue tracing back initiation however, those who write research proposals (such as faculty members) or stakeholders and funding organizations that write the call for proposals and policy documents to which they respond heavily influence this process. (Vines et al. 2013, p. 433)

The power to allocate resources and determine the skill composition of the team may rest in the project leader but it is driven by commitments of a variegated nature (e.g. agreed upon research objectives, a vision, the people and resources at hand). Not only that: some solutions have already been made material, hence difficult to neglect or 'undo' and therefore irreversible. The 'power of making', which is grounded in highly specialized skills and competencies, although potentially vulnerable, privileges designers' discourse in technical decisions. Moreover, power that is shared may in the end reside in the person who implements a decision, making it material: the trusted (or contested) expert. The power of users may also rest upon their 'material' ways of using a design or refusing to use it in the way that had been envisioned.

This leads to the observation that power is not the only mechanism regulating decision-making. Acting within a participatory framework and doing research requires argumentation and, ideally, participants strive for mutual understanding. In some decisions influence needs to be exerted more directly, as for example in negotiations with the outside world. Influence can be consensus-oriented, but it often has a strategic element and uses persuasion. We have shown how influence as a regulating mechanism is very common in decisions requiring highly specialized, mostly technical expertise. A large number of these decisions are also based on trust. Loyalty is another important concept in thinking about decision-making: some participants may keep their original loyalties while bringing in their perspectives to a project, without necessarily developing loyalties to the project team. There is also the phenomenon of divided or dual loyalties (Pedersen 2007), as in the case of professionals who may be 'torn' between their community of origin and the vision of a project that may introduce a novel form of practice. We also have seen in the case of a distributed designer team a conflict of loyalty between a highly sophisticated practice and one that may be less exciting but works in use (Bjerknes and Bratteteig 1988). Finally, there is the unconditional loyalty to the user group (children ill with cancer; normal citizens whose voice should be given space).

We have looked into issues of power/knowledge, coming to the conclusion that these are difficult to disentangle from other sources of power, in particular from how power is enacted. We have particularly examined how topics are constructed through 'discourse' and explored instances of 'normalising practices'. Some observations stand out clearly. For example, openness very much depends on the diversity and multiplicity of discourses that are 'admitted' in a project: they have an enormous influence on the design space. Restricting these voices to a few that look 'useful' from the beginning, leads to a narrowing down of the design space. 'Experience' (e.g. of a senior researcher) and the ability to 'speak' in different languages—in stories, in visual material, in the making—is also a powerful resource. Interestingly, specialized technical expertise, although not really accessible to non-engineers, can also be enormously vulnerable: things may not work and a solution may not be ready at hand. We have also seen some instances of the power of 'normalising'. This is most obvious in the case where standardized knowledge exists that is not easy to contest. However, in this case, the commitment to listening to how children speak, created another, partly competing sort of 'evidence'.

This type of power is much less easy to perceive and compensate when it comes to forms of expressing that demand a specific literacy: in our case visual material and sound, which have a 'manipulative potential'. The skilled use of images and sound may have a strong 'disciplining' effect (Robertson 2000) that excludes those who don't have the fluency and experience needed to skillfully use these means of expression.

References

Acker, J. (1992). Gendering organizational theory. In A. Mills & P. Tancred (Eds.), *Gendering organizational analysis* (pp. 248–260). Newbury Park: Sage.

Anderson, L. M., Mulligan, B. E., Goodman, L. S., & Regen, H. Z. (1983). Effects of sounds on preferences for outdoor settings. *Environment and Behavior, 15*(5), 539–566.

Barbalet, J. M. (1996). Social emotions: Confidence, trust and loyalty. *The International Journal of Sociology and Social Policy, 6*(9/10), 75–96.

Besley, T. (2005). Foucault, truth telling and technologies of the self in schools. *Journal of Educational Enquiry, 6*(1), 76–89.

Bjerknes, G., & Bratteteig, T. (1987). *Perspectives on description tools and techniques in system development*. Paper presented at the IFIP TC 9/WG 9.1 Working Conference on system design for human development and productivity: Participation and beyond Amsterdam.

Bjerknes, G., & Bratteteig, T. (1988). Computers—utensils or epaulets? The application perspective revisited. *AI & Society, 2*(3), 258–266.

Bjögvinsson, E., Ehn, P., & Hillgren, P.-A. (2012). Design things and design thinking: Contemporary participatory design challenges. *Design Issues, 28*(3), 101–116.

Borum, F., & Enderud, H. (1981). *Konflikter i organisationer: Belyst ved studier af edb-systemar-bejde (Conflicts in organisations, illustrated by cases of computer systems design)*. Copenhagen: Nyt Nordisk Forlag Arnold Busck.

Bourdieu, P. (1979). *La distinction. Critique sociale du jugement*. Paris: Éditions de Minuit, Le Sens commun.

Bowker, G., & Star, S. L. (1999). *Sorting things out. Classifications and its consequences*. Cambridge: MIT Press.

Bratteteig, T., & Wagner, I. (2012b). Spaces for participatory creativity. *CoDesign, 8*(2–3), 105–126.

Burrell, G. (1988). Modernism, post modernism and organizational analysis 2: The contribution of Michel Foucault. *Organization Studies, 9*, 221–235.

Butler, J. (1997). *The psychic life of power. Theories of subjection*. Stanford: Stanford University Press.

Carles, J. L., Barrio, I. L., & De Lucio, J. V. (1999). Sound influence on landscape values. *Landscape and Urban Planning, 43*(4), 191–200.

Cooper, D. (1994). Productive, relational and everywhere? Conceptualising power and resistance within Foucauldian feminism. *Sociology, 28*, 435–554.

Crozier, M. (1973). The problem of power. In M. Crozier (Ed.), *The stalemate society*. New York: The Viking Press.

Dahl, R. A. (1957). The concept of power. *Behavioral science, 2*(3), 201–215.

Day, R., & Day, J. A. (1977). A review of the current state of negotiated order theory: An appreciation and a critique. *Sociological Quarterly, 18*(1), 126–142.

Druin, A. (2002). The role of children in the design of new technology. *Behaviour and Information Technology, 21*(1), 1–25.

Dunn, J. (1990). Trust and political agency. In D. Gambetta (Ed.), *Trust: Making and breaking cooperative relations* (pp. 73–93). Oxford: Blackwell.

Elias, N. (1976). *Über den Prozeß der Zivilisation. Soziogenetische und psychogenetische Untersuchungen*. Frankfurt: Suhrkamp.

Estevez, D. (2001). *Dessin d'architecture et Infographie. L'évolution Contemporaine des Pratiques Graphiques*. Paris: CNRS. (In C. éditions (Ed.)).

Finken, S. (2005). *Methods as technologies for producing knowledge. An encounter with cultural practices—reflections from a field study in a high-tech company*. Roskilde: Roskilde University. (PhD).

Foucault, M. (1973). *The history of sexuality*. Harmondsworth: Penguin Books.

Foucault, M. (1979). *Discipline and punish: The birth of prison*. New York: Vintage Books.

Foucault, M. (1982). The subject and power. *Critical Inquiry, 8*(4), 777–795.

Foucault, M. (1988). Technologies of the self. In L. H. Martin, H. Gutman, & P. H. Hutton (Eds.), *Technologies of the self* (pp. 16–49). Amherst: University of Massachusetts Press.

Giddens, A. (1991). *The consequences of modernity*. Stanford: Stanford University Press.

Habermas, J. (1981). *Theorie des kommunikativen Handelns*. Frankfurt: Suhrkamp.

Hall, S. (1996). Who needs identity. *Questions of Cultural Identity, 16*(2), 1–17.

Hall, S. (1997). The work of representation. In S. Hall (Ed.), *Representation: Cultural representations and signifying practices*. London: Sage.

Hardy, C., & Clegg, S. (1996). Some dare call it power. In S. Clegg, C. Hardy, & W. Nord (Eds.), *Handbook of organizational studies* (pp. 622–641). London: Sage.

Hekman, S. (2010). *The material of knowledge. Feminist disclosures*. Bloomington: Indiana University Press.

Hyysalo, S., & Lehenkari, J. (2002). *Contextualizing power in a collaborative design*. Paper presented at the PDC 2002, Malmö.

Kanter, R. (1979). Power failure in management circuits. *Harvard Business Review, 57*(4), 65–75.

Lacan, J. (1979). *The four fundamental concepts of psychoanalysis*. Harmondsworth: Penguin.

Latour, B. (1986). Visualization and cognition: Thinking with eyes and hands. *Knowledge and Society: Studies in the Sociology of Culture Past and Present, 6*, 1–40.

Lemke, T. (2001). Max Weber, Norbert Elias und Michel Foucault über Macht und Subjektivierung. *Berliner Journal für Soziologie, 1*, 77–95.

Manning, S., & Sydow, J. (2011). Projects, paths, and practices: Sustaining and leveraging project-based relationships. *Industrial and Corporate Change, 20*(5), 1369–1402.

Marx, K., & Engels, F. (1848). *The communist manifesto*. New York: International Publishers.

Moldaschl, M. (2003). Foucaults Brille. Eine Möglichkeit, die Subjektivierung von Arbeit zu verstehen? In M. Moldaschl (Ed.), *Subjektivierung von Arbeit* (2nd ed., pp. 135–177). München: Hampp.

Morgan, G. (1986). *Images of organization*. London: Sage.

Neto, P. L. (2006). Public perception in contemporary Portugal: The digital representation of space. *Journal of Urban Design, 11*(3), 347–366.

Pedersen, J. (2007). Protocols of research and design. Reflections on a participatory design project (sort of). (PhD thesis), IT University, Copenhagen.

Pitkin, H. F. (1973). *Wittgenstein and justice*. Berkeley: University of California Press.

Rabaté, J.-M. (2003). *The Cambridge companion to Lacan*. Cambridge: Cambridge University Press.

Roberts, J. (2005). The power of the 'imaginary' in disciplinary processes. *Organization, 12*(5), 619–642.

Robertson, T. (2006). Ethical issues in interaction design. *Ethics and Information Technology, 8*(2), 49–59.

Rogan, B. (1992). Artefacts—source material or research objects in contemporary ethnology? *Ethnologia Scandinavica, 22*, 105–117.

Schmidt, K. (2011). *Cooperative work and coordinative practices*. New York: Springer.

Simonsen, J., & Kensing, F. (1994). *Take users seriously, but take a deeper look: Organizational and technical effects from designing with an ethnographically inspired approach*. Paper presented at the Participatory Design Conference PDC'94, Chapel Hill NC.

Söderstrom, O., & Zepf, M. (1998). L'image négociée. *disP-The Planning Review, 34*(134), 12–19.

Star, S. L., & Bowker, G. (2001). Enacting silence: Residual categories as a challenge for ethics, information systems, and communication. *Ethics and Information Technology, 9*, 273–280.

Stokes, J., & Clegg, S. (2002). Once upon a time in the bureaucracy: Power and public sector management. *Organization Science, 9*(2), 225–247.

Strauss, A. (1979). *Negotiations: Varieties, contexts, processes, and social order*. San Francisco: Jossey-Bass.

Suchman, L. (1994). Computer supported cooperative work. *Do categories have politics? 2*(3), 177–190.

Vines, J., Clarke, R., Wright, P., McCarthy, J., & Olivier, P. (2013). *Configuring participation: On how we involve people in design*. Paper presented at the Proceedings of the SIGCHI Conference on Human Factors in Computing Systems.

Wagner, I. (2000). *'Persuasive Artefacts' in architectural design and planning*. Paper presented at the Processings of CoDesigning, Nottingham.

Weber, M. (1978). *Economy and society: An outline of interpretive sociology*. New York: Wiley.

Weick, K. E. (1985). Sources of order in underorganized systems: Themes in recent organizational theory. In Y. S. Lincoln (Ed.), *Organizational theory and inquiry* (pp. 106–136). Beverly Hills: Sage.

Whitley, R. (2006). Project-based firms: New organizational form or variations on a theme? *Industrial and Corporate Change, 15*(1), 77–99.

Zündorf, L. (1986). Macht, Einfluß, Vertrauen und Verständigung. Zum Problem der Handlungskoordinierung in Arbeitsorganisationen. In R. Seltz, U. Mill, & E. Hildebrandt (Eds.), *Organisation als soziales system* (pp. 33–56). Berlin: Sigma.

Chapter 7
Participation

Giving a voice to users is a strong normative imperative in PD: it implies the responsibility of participatory designers to include users in all kinds of decisions. The roots of this imperative are a commitment to democratic values, such as equality, autonomy, democratic self-realization, self-organization, and solidarity, on the one hand. On the other hand involving users in the design of the technologies they will use is based on the premise that the outcomes of the design are more likely to be successful. The two projects we have analyzed have used participatory methods and techniques. However, the users did not have a say in all decisions. Hence, in this chapter we ask what it means to participate.

7.1 What is Participation?

Participation is defined as the action or fact of having or forming part of something or the sharing of something (Oxford English Dictionary). In general, participation refers to the process of decision-making, in which lay people express their opinions and influence the decisions. The World Bank offers this definition: 'Participation is a process through which stakeholders influence and share control over development initiatives and the decisions and resources which affect them' (The World Bank 1994). Participation presupposes that the decision-making process is transparent to some extent and open for the participants to be present. In addition, as a prerequisite for participating, all participants need to have information that is understandable and timely.

A more 'political' view on participation looks at it as a means to 'increase the involvement of socially and economically marginalized people in decision-making over their own lives' (Guijt and Shah 1998, p. 1). 'Marginalized' refers to people who are normally not part of decision-making in design. Depending on the context, this may be patients, old and frail people, children or people who are poor and /or live in poor countries, and so forth. With respect to the design of future IT systems or products, also users that are not socially and economically disadvantaged may be considered marginalized, as they normally are not part of decision-making in design.

T. Bratteteig, I. Wagner, *Disentangling Participation,* Computer Supported
Cooperative Work, DOI 10.1007/978-3-319-06163-4_7,
© Springer International Publishing Switzerland 2014

The notion of participation is key to a variety of engagements, such as community development, health care, architecture, town planning and agricultural development (Harder et al. 2013). Some of the literature in these fields aims at disentangling the notion of participation. We start with Pretty who mentions 'two overlapping schools':

> One views participation as a means to increase efficiency, the central notion being that if people are involved, then they are more likely to agree with and support the new development and service. The other sees participation as a fundamental right, in which the main aim is to initiate mobilization for collective action, empowerment and institution building. (Pretty 1995, p. 1251)

Given the wide range of motivations and aims, it seems that there is not one shared view of participation and that there are even contradictory assumptions about what it means to participate: 'An infinitely malleable concept, "participation" can be used to evoke—and to signify—almost anything that involves people' (Cornwall 2008, p. 269).

Participation implies influence, which can be defined as effect or the capacity to have an effect, where effect refers to a change resulting from an action that brings it about. From this we take that participation leads to change. We have made the distinction between influence and power, although some situations may involve both; and also differentiated between influence that is strategic and achievement-oriented or more consensus-oriented. The latter form of influence is based on the ability to convince and persuade (Zündorf 1986, p. 37).

In characterizing participation, much of the literature mixes personal, processual and product-related aspects. The maybe most well-known categorization is Arnstein's who suggests a 'ladder' with eight 'rungs' characterizing 'the extent of citizens' power in determining the "end product"' (Arnstein 1969, p. 216) (Fig. 7.1). Arnstein's concern is that '"nobodies" … are trying to become "somebodies" with enough power to make the target institutions responsive to their views, aspirations and needs' (ibid, p. 217): the ladder tells how well they succeed. She draws a distinction between empowering forms of participation, 'tokenism' (in which she includes consultation, informing and placation) and nonparticipation. The ladder reflects Dahl's classic definition of power as 'power over'—to affect the behavior of others, prompting a person 'to do something he would not otherwise do' (Dahl 1957, p. 202). Arnstein's ladder mixes the type, scope and experience of participation.

Also Gaventa refers to the purpose of the process leading to different types or degrees of participation:

- *Manipulation or co-optation,* e.g. to support the status quo, and to divert opposing voices,
- *Legitimacy,* e.g. to insure wider ownership and support for an agenda which already has been pre-determined, or which will really be decided elsewhere,
- *Efficiency,* e.g. to help make projects or programmes more cost-effective, targeted and sustainable,
- *Transformation,* to change underlying social and power relations in favour of the poor and previously excluded (Gaventa 2006, p. 14).

Fig. 7.1 Arnstein's 'ladder of participation'

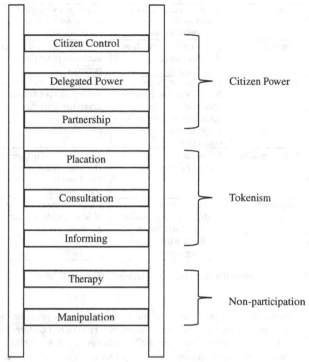

Gaventa points to the fact that power is not problematized in the three first forms of participation. He also stresses that these purposes are not mutually exclusive: different actors may engage in a participatory process with any of these aims in mind. In fact, some of the literature uses the notion of 'depth' of participation, which refers to the extent of control over decision-making, thus addressing power issues (Harder et al. 2013).

Pretty suggests a typology similar to Arnstein's ladder, although seen from the participant position (Pretty 1995). His typology reaches from 'manipulative participation', where 'participation is simply a pretense', to self-mobilization. He introduces a distinction between participation as a means (functional participation) and participation as a right (interactive participation), where the process is a joint effort. Both, Arnstein's and Pretty's, typologies describe

> a spectrum defined by a shift from control by authorities to control by the people or citizens.
> Yet the end-points are rather different. … What Pretty's typology helps make clear is that
> the motivations of those who adopt and practise participatory approaches is an important
> factor … in shaping interventions. And what Arnstein's reminds us is that participation is
> ultimately about power and control. (Cornwall 2008, p. 271)

A similar typology is suggested by Cornwall who adds the dimension of how participation is seen by the participants, as well as by the 'implementing agency'. Her 'typology of interests' (Fig. 7.2), which she has adapted from White (1996), focuses on who participates and where their agency and their interests take them. Cornwall stresses:

Form	What 'participation' means to the implementing agency	What 'participation' means for those on the receiving end	What 'participation' for
Nominal	Legitimation – to show they are doing something	Inclusion – to retain some access to potential benefits	Display
Instrumental	Efficiency – to limit funder's input, draw on community contributions and make projects more cost-effective	Cost – of time spent on project-related labour and other activities	As a means to achieving cost-effectiveness and local facilities
Representative	Sustainability – to avoid creating dependency	Leverage – to influence the shape the project takes and its management	To give people a voice in determining their own development
Transformative	Empowerment – to enable people to make their own decisions, work out what to do and take action	Empowerment – to be able to decide and act for themselves	Both as a means and an end, a continuing dynamic

Fig. 7.2 Cornwall's 'typology of interests'. (Cornwall 2008)

> Participation as praxis is, after all, rarely a seamless process; rather, it constitutes a terrain of contestation, in which relations of power between different actors, each with their own 'projects', shape and reshape the boundaries of action. While a frame might be set by outsiders, much then depends on *who* participates and where *their* agency and interests take things'. (Cornwall 2008, p. 276)

With her typology Cornwall refers to a set of generalized interests, such as inclusion, cost-effectiveness, and leverage. In the context of a PD project participants' interests are usually much more specific, depending on the objectives of the project and the choices that open up. Moreover, they may be overlapping and/or in conflict with each other; and they may not be so clear.

In response to Arnstein's 'ladder of participation' Rocha has defined a 'ladder of empowerment' (Rocha 1967). Empowerment has a slightly different meaning. To 'empower' means 'to give official or legal power or authority, to endow with an ability or to enable' (Rodwell 1996, p. 306). It points to the person rather than the result of the process. Participation is often supposed to lead to some form of empowerment, giving ordinary people agency. However, as Cornwall and Brock critically remark 'empowerment retains a prominent place in agencies' policies concerning gender, but often appears in a diluted form, neutralizing its original emphasis on building personal and collective power in the struggle for a more just and equitable world' (Cornwall and Brock 2005, p. 1046).

The context of Rocha's thinking is town planning. The types of empowerment are based on the 'power experience' of participants, a notion that has been developed by McClelland (McClelland 1975). Rocha constructs a four-cell typology based on the source and object of power—both distinguishing between self and other (Fig. 7.3). The experience of power develops in fours stages, introducing progress into the discussion of empowerment. In the first stage the participant gains

Fig. 7.3 Experiences of power after McClelland 1975. (Rocha 1967)

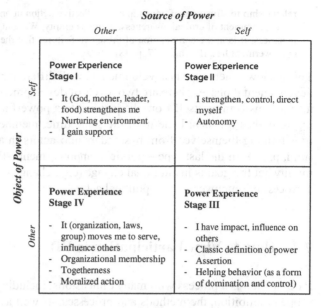

<table>
<tr><td colspan="3" align="center">Source of Power</td></tr>
</table>

	Other	Self
Self	**Power Experience Stage I** - It (God, mother, leader, food) strengthens me - Nurturing environment - I gain support	**Power Experience Stage II** - I strengthen, control, direct myself - Autonomy
Other	**Power Experience Stage IV** - It (organization, laws, group) moves me to serve, influence others - Organizational membership - Togetherness - Moralized action	**Power Experience Stage III** - I have impact, influence on others - Classic definition of power - Assertion - Helping behavior (as a form of domination and control)

Object of Power (vertical axis label)

power from associating with a strong 'other'. In the second stage the participant obtains autonomy—i.e. what we described as 'power to'. Stage three in the model concerns having impact—or influence—where Rocha also includes helping others. Stage four looks beyond the individual to the collective, feeling powerful by serving principles.

Based on these distinctions, Rocha develops a five-step ladder of empowerment. The three first steps concern the 'power experience of those becoming empowered' (Rocha 1967, p. 37). This focus on the participating individual is important. It directs attention to the fact that individual users may benefit from participating in a PD project by gaining skills and competencies—the 'strength is gained from the support of powerful others' (ibid, p. 34). Participation may also strengthen the individual's feeling of autonomy in a particular context, through being a member and also through participating in decision-making in this particular context. The power experience also depends on whether expert guidance is needed to support an individual's 'ability to exercise choice'. Rocha stresses that a good working relationship between a layperson and an expert can be empowering, provided that both resist 'the pressure to succumb to a mode of interaction that may invalidate a truly empowering process' (ibid, p. 37).

The last two types in Rocha's 'ladder'—socio-political and political empowerment—focus on community development (the locus is community) through changing the people who belong to it. The basis for this type is Freire's 'pedagogy of the oppressed' (Freire 1970): 'To Freire, community empowerment starts when people listen to each other, engage in participatory/liberatory dialogue, identify their commonalities, and construct new strategies for change' (Wallerstein and Bernstein 1994, p. 143). The process that leads to empowerment includes critical reflection about the community members' relationship to structures of power and … collective action upon those structures. Without the development of critical awareness, action is empty. Without action, critical awareness is useless. It is in the combination of these two features that the strength of this model of empowerment lies. (Rocha 1967, p. 38)

This empowerment type is developmental, with different power experiences in each developmental phase. There are two levels of development involved: 'The community is transforming itself from the inside into a powerful actor, capable of garnering resources for local benefit; at the same time, members-of-the-community are transforming themselves from bystanders into actors in and through this process' (ibid, p. 38). In the last type—political empowerment—the locus is also the community but the goal is institutional change (e.g., change of legislation) by means of a process of empowerment as political action.

7.2   How to View Participation in PD

Participation is a process with many dimensions, including the purpose or goal, the scope or ambition, the methods and processes, as well as the power experience of the participants. The purposes and interests that participants bring into a PD project may be multiple and rather varied.

Cornwall warns against reading typologies such as the ones we discuss here as progressing towards more 'genuine' forms of participation, arguing:

When these forms of participation are contextualized, however, they become more ambiguous. … But keeping a flow of information going is in itself important, rather than being simply a 'lesser' form of participation … And … even the most nominal forms of participation can give citizens a foot in the door if there has been no constructive engagement with them before. (Cornwall 2008, p. 272 f.)

Hence, the ideal of 'full participation' cannot be the one and only measure of how participatory a project has been. There is the need to consider the many dimensions of a PD project to be able to evaluate how participatory it was.

In the literature on participation we normally find questions about who participates, questioning the representativity of participants and their specific roles. There may be quite subtle mechanisms that limit participation, as in the case of social and cultural differences that make it difficult to have one's voice heard. Cornwall also points at self-exclusion that

can be associated with a lack of confidence, with the experience of being silenced by more powerful voices or fear of reprisals. It can be because people feel that they have nothing to contribute, that their knowledge and ideas are more likely to be laughed at than taken seriously. (Cornwall 2008, p. 278)

Thus the space for participation becomes interesting: who provides the space, and who invites the participants. Gaventa is more precise when asking: 'Whose *voices* are heard? Who created the *space*? For what *purpose* is the participation being promoted? Whose *power* is affected by it?' (Gaventa 2006, p. 12). These questions go deeper in exploring how participation is enacted by looking at the participants, the characteristics of the space, in which participation takes place, the purpose, as well as the participatory result.

We find that even if many authors ask these questions, they seldom answer them in a concrete and precise way. We hear about who the participants are but rarely about their competencies (Kanstrup and Christiansen 2006 being an exception). Most of the literature describes how the PD methods and techniques were tailored, modified or combined to suit the particular context of a project, so as to engage the participants. But engagement is not necessarily participation. What is seldom discussed are the objectives of the participatory effort, as if the participatory process were the goal itself; nor is the 'system success' examined as a participatory result. The power issues in the participatory project (or its results) are rarely addressed in the PD literature; much more so in the more general literature on participation.

What remains unclear is what exactly it is that participants influence and how they recognize their influence. Let us take a look at the decisions taken in *IPCity* and *Sisom* to see if we can get closer to these questions:

> To speak of 'involving people in decision-making' implies that all and any decisions are up for grabs. Yet, it is important to be clear about exactly *which* decisions the public have the opportunity to participate in, and indeed *which* members of the public participate in different kinds of decision-making fora. On closer inspection, claims to have 'involved the public' may boil down to having a few conversations with a couple of community leaders or calling people to a public meeting, which only the most active members of a community attend. (Cornwall 2008, p. 280)

In the following sections we take a step further in our analysis, taking up the different dimensions of participation the literature discusses and going back to the different kinds of decisions taken in the two projects and their linkages. Three leading questions structure this analysis:

- Who was involved?
- In which choices were participants involved and how did they participate in the decision-making?
- How participatory were the design results and what kinds of decisions made them participatory?

7.3   Who was Involved?

Let us first look at stakeholder participation, which framed both projects from the beginning. Both projects worked with more than one group of users: urban planners and 'normal' citizens in the case of *IPCity*; children and health care personnel in the case of *SiSom*.

In *IPCity* the 'depth of participation' was different for these different types of participants. The project had been organized to have urban specialists participate as full partners in the whole design process. They surely represented an important group of users. The rationale behind this decision was that they would be those most likely to also in the future organize urban projects in a more participatory way, including citizens and other stakeholders. This is a role they fulfilled in the project when they negotiated with the 'owners' of urban projects to open up to experimenting with participatory tools with real stakeholders. As we saw, the French urban planner team had influence on choices on three levels: on the design of the *ColorTable*, in particular the functionalities; on how to represent an urban project (panoramas as representations of a site, content to work with); and on the selection of particular urban projects for participatory workshops.

That citizens were not involved to the same extent has to do with the approach of the project. Had the project leader opted for collaborating with one particular urban project over the course of several years, the team may have had the opportunity to involve a group of citizens in a more continuous way. Hence, the project would have been 'more participatory' towards this user group. However, arranging for such long-term participation was not considered feasible. Not only for lack of resources: it would have required successfully negotiating citizens' time away from work and other important activities, including some compensation for the work they contributed with. We think, however, that it would have been unrealistic to count on a long-term commitment of 'normal' citizens in *IPCity*. We contend that the nature and time-scale of urban projects is unfavorable to the full time participation of people who are not involved in the planning on a professional level. Hence, a selection of citizens only participated in one or at most two of the workshops with the power to appropriate the tools and engage with them in their own ways.

The selection of workshop participants had to be negotiated with urban project owners and local authorities. It turned out to be a rather sensitive political issue, since municipalities feared having to include critical views. Projects like these run the risk that participants representing important but peripheral voices and/or from whose contribution a project would greatly benefit cannot even be identified and 'found'. An interesting question is if the visions created by the workshop participants had any influence on the urban projects they engaged with. Although the urban team conducted feedback sessions with the 'owners' of both projects in Cergy-Pontoise this is hard to tell, given the complexity and 'longue durée' of these projects and the fact that the workshops were just one intervention in a long process.

In *SiSom* the participating children did not have as much influence on the design result as the urban specialists in *IPCity*, but more than the workshop participants. The children had an important voice as 'informants', as experts on 'how children think'; and as 'testers', contributing to some choices and removing others (e.g. 'a game is too childish for such a serious situation'). The children acted as substitutes for children with cancer. But this was a world not really accessible to them and which they could just try to imagine as best as possible.

There is an ethical dimension to the well-know representativity problem in PD:

> The ethical issue that arises here is not only how to make limitations to participation transparent but how to make the decision on where the limitation comes in and why: is the limitation due to legal constraints or costs; is it due to medical concerns; or is it just simpler working with healthy children? (Robertson and Wagner 2012, p. 73)

In the case of *Sisom* the limitation was clearly due to medical concerns: the medical staff had advised against including cancer patients. They thought them to be too weak and vulnerable to be included in the workshops. Moreover, patients often don't stay long enough in hospital to be available for an extended period. Hence, the most vulnerable stakeholders were protected; healthy children tried to imagine their situation without being able to fully capture their views and experiences.

7.4 Participation in Different Kinds of Decisions

The case of *SiSom* is special, as the main users were children. It was the project leader who had envisioned and defined the project. She was committed to improving the treatment of severely ill children; moreover, she aligned the project with the evidence-based medical tradition to get acceptance in the hospital context. The children participated in the two key elements of the design: the navigation mechanism and the building of the vocabulary. However, the ways they were invited to contribute were carefully designed.

Decisions concerning the vision as well as how to implement it were taken in very similar ways, by the project leader and the core team. The basis for the decisions was professional competence concerning children with cancer. Although the role of the children in the *Sisom* design process looks similar to that of the citizens in *IPCity*: influencing basically through use or non-use, the children's ideas were more systematically considered as choices to be included into the decision-making process. All workshops with children were video-recorded. The team watched these videos afterwards selecting ideas they thought were interesting. These ideas were then 'polished' by a graphic designer to return to the children as beautiful and finished. Hence, children were 'seduced' into making or confirming certain choices. Ruland et al. explain their approach as follows:

> Good design for ill children requires knowledge, and pedagogical, psychological and clinical insights children don't have. In our work we had to make sure to meet the goals of SISOM and a set of pre-defined criteria. Especially, we had to ensure to design software that could help children to report their symptoms and problem experiences, without being too time-consuming and challenging. Not all of the children's ideas were therefore, feasible. Our children participants often suggested fun and time-consuming aspects, such as funny noises along with vivid animations for a symptom such as throwing up. In spite of reminders that we were not designing a game, the children had the tendency to slip back into a 'game mode'. Also, children could spend considerable time on fine details and lose sight of the overall purpose. (Ruland et al. 2008, p. 634)

We note that the evaluation of the children's design moves was done by the adult participants, which made the design workshops appear similar to school—with school-like roles and power distribution. Limiting children's influence was based on the assumption that they do not have sufficient insight and may focus on aspects that are fun but peripheral from a professional perspective. Hence, their design moves were carefully restrained by 'a set of predefined criteria' that were to ensure the goals of *SiSom*.

While the decision to use islands as the main navigation mechanism was taken very early (by the project leader, based on the pilot the children liked), several smaller decisions about navigation in each island were taken later, by the project leader and her core team, based on a rather selective approach to the childrens' design suggestions. The children's drawings were used as a source of inspiration rather than as concrete choices.

The 'vocabulary' for talking about symptoms was not built bottom-up through, for example, listening to how ill children talk about their symptoms. The children worked with a list of symptoms that already had been viewed and modified by nurses, doctors, psychologists, and parents. The final decision about how to translate the pre-given vocabulary into the language of children was in their hands (see Table 3.1): their expertise in this matter was held unquestionable.

The decision, in which situations to use the *Sisom* system was not participatory, neither was the question about the representativity of the children. However, testing was done by leaving the system with ill children at the hospital ward:

> It was preferable that the child would complete Sisom with as little interference as possible. Most children used headphones so that nobody else could hear the voice and sound in the program, and almost all children completed Sisom on their own. (Vatne et al. 2013, p. 3)

The children were free to use the system in the way they wanted—and it turned out that the expectation about its use and usefulness were more than fulfilled.

Sisom was designed as a sequence of linked decisions, and was experienced in this way by the adult participants. There were some occurrences of sequential linkages that also the children noticed, as they worked on a series of steps in the design process. But the decisions were not taken by them. The decision to make islands be the major navigation metaphor opened up for several decisions about the navigation on each island—but it was not clear to the children that this was how the final design was decided. Lateral linkages and also precursive linkages were not visible to the children participants, hence the effects of their contributions (and possible decisions) were not understood. We might say that the children were delivering ideas and choices to the project, but that the selection between the choices and their further development were done by the adult participants alone.

Also *IPCity* was framed by the commitment to creating a participatory tool. The vision of how to achieve this was based in field studies of architectural practice that had led the participatory designer to think of 'openness' as a basic characteristic of good design. From her research came the idea of what would support participation in urban planning: to be able to co-construct a vision of a site and immediately see the results. The urban planner team agreed with this vision, although the notion of 'immediacy' appeared strange to them, as architects mainly use drawings and simulation software. Agreeing on the vision was possible since previous interactions had helped establish common interests and mutual respect. This consensus was strengthened by the fact that urban planners' expertise in defining how to represent an urban site, based on 'urban concepts' was never questioned. Despite of what appeared as a common basis, much of the work in *IPCity* turned out to be 'proof of concept', with the materialization of the concept in an evolving set of prototypes

Fig. 7.4 The two objects (parking for cars and bikes) that had been placed in the aerial view appear as towering over the landscape in the panorama view

being constantly contested by the urban team who found it difficult to accept the imperfections of the prototypes. Participation took the form of a 'balancing act' between different interpretations of the vision.

Participation in decisions on how to implement this vision shows a different pattern. To work with photographic panoramas of a site was stimulated by participants in the first workshop in Sainte-Anne who were interested in a representation that would allow them 'walk around'. We have seen that this choice 'evoked' a series of related decisions. Here the urban planners took the lead, insisting on modeling the panoramas so as to support placing objects 'correctly' with attention to height and volume and to handle occlusion properly. The right scale and exact positioning of objects was one of the basic requirements from the beginning: it was considered a prerequisite for an architectural argument.

The workshop participants, however, did not focus so much on precision. They were good at coping with the imperfections of, for example, the photographic panoramas: sizing and arranging objects 'optically' in relation to other objects; adapting to the fact that objects' position and sizes did not remain stable when switching representation, e.g. from a photographic panorama to a real-time video view of the site. They tended to look at interventions as 'symbolic' rather than realistic. A telling example is shown in Fig. 7.4, in which two large objects towering over a landscape can be seen. The participants in the workshop in Pontoise had placed these objects before using an areal view of the site. When they switched to the panorama view of the site, these objects suddenly appeared much larger. Participants were surprised by this effect, but pleased with the impact of what they interpreted as a symbolic intervention. They understood that what they co-constructed was open and 'fuzzy' (in the language of architects). They did not see the need for precision at the stage of vision building. This is a moment in which the 'seeing' of 'normal' citizens clashed with the 'seeing' of professional architects. The choice of the non-expert users strengthened the designers' decision not to prioritize 'precision'.

However, the 'new visual language', the project aimed at, remained contested until the end of the project. We already described that translating content from cultural probes to 'content cards' to be used on the *ColorTable* was only partially successful. The visual experience of the artist was not respected in the same way as technical or architectural expertise. Participation in the selection of content was strong, as participants were free to choose content that appealed to them, rejecting some of the carefully prepared material. At the same time, the artist had a strong role in the project, as her effort at editing visual material enabled participants to create rich mixed reality scenes representing their ideas.

In contrast to visual content that evoked divergent 'opinions', working with sound turned out a collaborative struggle. The problems to be solved here were not technical but conceptual. Most of the work was done by the sound specialist in the team, an active musician, in collaboration with the artist. As a powerful software (*Ambisonics*) for positioning sound spatially in a 360° sound field existed, both focused on producing probes of ambient sound that represented the themes selected for a workshop; on connecting sound with particular visual content; and also on capturing the sound typical of different photographic panoramas. While this work was largely artistic, it was influenced by a series of interviews with sound specialists, who addressed questions such as: how to categorize the informative content of sound; how to evaluate and describe the personal and cultural meanings of sound; differences between realistic and abstract-synthetic sounds, between simulation and expressive uses of sound; how many sound strands users can handle, and so forth. Hence, working with sound was an issue that required outside expertise. Moreover, the sound application was quite 'vulnerable' as workshop participants found it difficult to integrate the sound into their scenarios and visions, simply for a general lack of experience. In the case of sound it was mainly the lack of competence that put limits to participation. No space was made for participants to develop such competence.

Bringing mixed reality outdoors had been a central element of the proposal. It defined a major research challenge for all. 'Nested' in this decision was the choice of the tracking mechanism, which had a 'precursive linkage' with the color tokens as key elements of the haptic interface. The development of the tracking mechanism was considered a more or less 'pure' engineering task. We already described the decisions concerning color tracking and its optimization. It was the designer team who introduced color tracking and developed it together with the maker of the algorithm. The possibilities for non-engineers to participate in these decisions were rather limited: participation consisted in working with the *ColorTable*, in communicating annoyance (with its instability), and in formulating priorities of the kind 'this has to be resolved urgently before we can take the *MR-Tent* to a new site'.

When looked upon it from the perspective of the engineers developing the artifact was not so straightforward and not a 'pure' engineering tasks. It involved a va-

Fig. 7.5 Different types of visual feedback: **a** marking detected shapes and colors with projected frame; **b** numerical information visible in projection; **c** 'info screen' with details about objects in the scene

riety of steps and was carried out in cycles. The engineers defined the requirements for tracking in collaboration with a researcher from Alborg University, who developed and gradually adapted a (rather too) powerful algorithm. This algorithm was imported and tested in an iterative process. Each time this involved three steps: first, the engineers tested the 'machinery', probing if its execution had the desired results. They then tested the artifact—the prototype of *ColorTable*—in the lab space. This required controlling for the lighting conditions, which should be as close as possible to those in the *MR-Tent*, and calibrating the colors of the tokens. Finally, the artifact was tested in use with practitioners. The colors of the tokens had to be calibrated again as soon as the *MR-Tent* had been set up and had to be recalibrated whenever weather conditions were changing:

> The well-known problem of changing lighting conditions turned out to be much more complex as assumed before. After using our system during a whole day, with an alternating number of users, the conditions considerably changed compared to other tests in the lab. In addition to the modifications due to the weather and daytime, lighting conditions were influenced by the participants themselves and by the angle or distance of their surface to the projector. (Maquil 2010, p. 73)

The developer from Alborg was present in all urban workshops, taking notes and assessing the problematic situations together with the Viennese designer team. In the end she found out that she had only fully understood the requirements when she finally used the tool herself, which was in one of the last workshops. Interestingly, no one had been aware of the fact that she simply had been too shy to ask, with everyone focusing on the workshop participants trying to respond to difficulties as they arose.

How participatory were these technical decisions? For the engineers considering real use, preparing for it and observing were indispensable. Just to give the example of 'feedback', which is a challenge in haptic user interfaces (Fig. 7.5):

> Depending on the topics of discussion, participants referred to results shown as numerical data (e.g. while scaling according to the own knowledge), illustrations (e.g. while setting streets) or the perspective view (e.g. while adjusting the position of objects). To support these diverse types of feedback, a certain amount of screens and projections is necessary. (Maquil 2010, p. 135)

Looking back at these choices and their consequences allows us better understand the power of users that may seem rather limited. In PD the design moves Schön describes are done collaboratively. Workshop participants actively participated in the 'seeing' part after a move: they selected (and ignored) content to work with; they tried hard to perform well at the *ColorTable*, allowing designers to learn how to improve the interaction design; they were active in the handling of some of the shortcomings of the representations of the site; they met the instability of tracking, which was at the edge of not meeting expectations, with stoicism most of the time.

7.5 How Participatory were the Design Results?

Evaluating how participatory a design project is requires also looking at the design result. This point has been made by several researchers. For example, Balka points to the importance of increasing the focus on the outcomes of PD projects, asking 'can we have good participatory processes that do not show evidence of more democratic ideals in the resulting artefacts?' (Balka 2010, p. 79). In their 'Foucault-inspired' analysis of a collaborative design project, Hyysalo and Lehenkari, following the making of diabetes databases in several hospitals, contend

> that it may be difficult for the participants in PD and cooperative projects to recognize the contextual dynamics that are at play within particular users, organization and technology production constellations. In other words, there is no guarantee that democratic participation can reveal and balance wider, historically·formed power structures affecting a design project, or that formal agreements help in preventing unwanted effects. (Hyysalo and Lehenkari 2002, p. 101 f)

Unrecognized power structures may prevent the design result from being participatory.

The design result of the *Sisom* project was (and still continues to be) participatory in a variety of ways. It presents a child's logic of talking about experienced symptoms. It gives children a voice in consultations with a doctor they would not have without the tool. They can use a language that is close to their own. This increases their influence on what is taken into consideration when doctors make choices about further treatment. Furthermore, 'when the child has visited all the islands, a child-friendly report that summarizes the child's reported problems is displayed and can be printed' (Ruland et al. 2008, p. 632). This means that the child's version of its illness is documented and becomes part of the patient record.

However, a child could not have imagined a tool such as *Sisom*. Adults were needed to conceptualize the tool and take care of all its features. Still, the participatory features of *Sisom* would not have been possible without the children's participation. They were the only ones capable of choosing the adequate expression of symptoms. They brought the gaming element to the attention of the project team, although the adults dismissed notions, such as 'shooting', as inadequate and games in general as not serious enough. In the end, the idea of 'islands' introduced gamification (rather than a game) into the system (Sending 2006). It allowed the children to report on their symptoms without having to follow a sequence, such as a list. This option stimulated a playful, explorative mode of use.

'Openness' lies at the heart of the *ColorTable* as a participatory tool. Observations of the *ColorTable* in use showed that the table acted as a mediator insofar as participants do not have to discuss in a confrontational way face-to-face but by means of gesturing, setting interventions, commenting, and modifying; and this in a mode of expression, which is not the expert's language. Erickson, among others, stresses the 'roughness' of design representations that leave openings for discussion (Erickson 1995). Another participatory feature was 'immediacy'—the possibility of doing and seeing the results of your actions. Participants did not have to wait for an expert to provide a drawing and an interpretation. The tool supports an inclusive mode of debating and co-constructing, which does not favor the expert. It leaves space for everybody.

> Another crucial fact was that the technical solution itself was relatively open: We did not implement any 'rules' or 'constraints' beyond the technical limitations of the tools, and with this made an explicit step away from simulation tools. This moved decisions away from the technology into the responsibility of the participants'. (Wagner et al. 2009, p. 193)

In fact, different groups of participants used the *ColorTable* in rather different ways. One of our observations on 'how creativity emerges from a multiplicity of contributing actors' was: 'participants with "real stakes" steered the discussion into solving problems, while those with more (professional or emotional) distance were more explorative' (Bratteteig and Wagner 2012, p. 122).

The role of citizens in urban projects is in general rather narrow, even if participatory processes have been set up. Citizens are usually limited to an oppositional role, voicing concerns. The *ColorTable* allows them move from a passive-critical to a constructive role: they are invited to imagine but they also learn to observe some of the rules of urban design. The fact that they have to cooperatively build a vision of the future of an urban site, making it concrete, makes them become part of a compromise.

Would the *ColorTable* have developed into a participatory tool without the participation of users? Well, the urban planners' voice was crucial, as they taught the team how to represent an urban site and how to define the key urban issues at stake, translating them into features of the tool. They also were to some extent open to breaking with the representational tradition of architecture. The workshop participants confirmed the design concept for *IPCity*. Their explorations of the *ColorTable* demonstrated how valuable it was to immediately see the results of a design move on the table, as well as in the projected mixed-reality scene; how important to have multiple representations of a site (physical map, panoramas from different viewpoints, real-time video) available for viewing a mixed reality scene (Wagner 2011); how well participants responded to the symbolic and fuzzy nature of the visual language the *ColorTable* provided. Moreover, the workshop participants' doing and seeing influenced the re-design moves that followed each workshop.

7.6 Summary

In the debate of PD and its methods a strong link between process and result is assumed: a participatory process is expected to lead to a participatory result. This is not always the case (Bjerknes and Bratteteig 1995). We have explored this assumption, looking into the kinds of decisions in both projects and into what the participants participated in and how. We think of a participatory result as one that increases users' 'power to'. The projects provide two different examples of 'power-to', each of which is about giving a voice: to citizen in urban projects; to ill children in consultations with doctors.

We have shown that not all decisions in a PD project have to be made in a participatory way. Even when choices are open to participation and all voices are heard, not all positions can be equally reflected in the design. Participation does not entail that all participants see their own particular contribution in the design result.

In both projects the vision did not come from future users but from the project leaders, based on previous research and a strong ethical stand. Also the purpose and method of participation had been defined in advance: to have users contribute to designing a participatory design result by involving them in different roles. In *IPCity* the expert-users had a strong voice in all choices but not necessarily an interest in participating in all of them. In the *Sisom* project the participation of children as experts was carefully designed and limited.

In both projects, many of the technical choices were not made in a participatory way. However, for both designer teams considering real use, preparing for it and observing it were indispensable. They also needed the support of the 'observers'— urban planners, and ethnographers—for interpreting the observations and coming to the 'right decisions'. This also holds true for the ill children who used *Sisom* while being in the hospital ward. We conclude from this that users strongly participate in the 'seeing' part of design moves, actively contributing to how a system is evaluated, which choices are supported and further developed and which not.

When looking at decision-making in both projects, an important aspect comes to the fore. We have seen in both projects users contribute to the creation of choices. In *IPCity* urban planners' expertise opened up for a whole range of choices on how to represent an urban project. The ways workshop participants used the *ColorTable* widened or modified a series of design choices. Also in *Sisom* the children's drawings created choices. Understanding how participants contribute to widening the design space provides one important perspective on participation. Some of the choices would not be present in decision-making without the contributions of the users.

Participation in decision-making, that is to say selecting among choices, is the other perspective to be examined. In *IPCity* only the urban experts users were directly involved in decision-making. Their status and role in the project made it impossible not to hear their voice. Their participation in decision-making was particularly strong concerning issues that were of key importance to them: which issues to address in an urban project. Participating in making a choice that then is implemented and evaluated is different from selecting how to use the different features of the *ColorTable*. Hence, participating in the 'seeing' is a weaker form of participation then having a say in a design choice, since it was up to the designer team to decide how they would work with observations from use. In *Sisom* the children decided on the 'vocabulary', based on a list that had been prepared by experts (and parents). But the project leader made all the selections among choices and also framed the process of making choices.

We conclude from these observations that within one and the same project there may be different depths of participation, depending on the role and particular expertise of participants but also on the types of issues. We have identified instances of consultation as well as real partnership in both projects (Arnstein 1969); certainly not mere informing or placation. Some of the power in decision-making was delegated to the 'expert users': the urban specialists in *IPCity*, the medical staff in *Sisom*. As concerns the purposes of participation (Gaventa 2006), legitimacy and efficiency, in the sense of including the expertise necessary for developing a good design were important motivations. Transformation, 'to change underlying social and power relations in favour of the poor and previously excluded' (ibid, p. 14) is visible in the design result itself, rather than in the decision-making process.

A crucial element of our view on participation is that the results of a project are participatory. In both cases we could see that some of the participatory features of the design results would not have been possible to imagine and design without the participation of users. Hence, the purpose of both projects was also to create a 'transformative result'.

As regards the 'power experience' of participants (Rocha 1967), we have not analyzed what individual participants gained from participation in the project, although 'what can PD offer participants' is an important ethical aspect (Robertson and Wagner 2012). As a participating collective both groups, the children and the workshop participants, experienced 'empowerment' in the sense of being invited to reflect and contribute in ways that would not have been feasible for them otherwise. The design of the six workshops in *Sisom* reflects the development of 'power experience' (McClelland 1975), with some of the children arriving at what McClelland terms 'feeling powerful by serving principles' (Fig. 5.3). In *IPCity* workshop participants experienced to be able to contribute to an urban project on equal footing with the experts, with arguments and choices that changed the view of the participating urban planners. In both projects participants felt that they represented others. This opened a new way of thinking about their contribution: helping severely ill children to report their symptoms; making marginal voices heard in an urban planning project.

Our conclusion, which we will elaborate in the last chapter, is that there is not one single measure of participation in PD. Participation is a multifaceted process and experience: there is not one 'right way'. But some things are more important than others.

References

Arnstein, S. R. (1969). A ladder of citizen participation. *Journal of the American Institute of Planners, 35*(4), 216–224.

Balka, E. (2010). Broadening discussion about participatory design. *Scandinavian Journal of Information Systems, 22*(1), 77–84.

Bjerknes, G., & Bratteteig, T. (1995). User participation and democracy. A discussion of Scandinavian research on systems development. *Scandinavian Journal of Information Systems, 7*(1), 73–98.

Bratteteig, T., & Wagner, I. (2012). Spaces for participatory creativity. *CoDesign, 8*(2–3), 105–126.

Cornwall, A. (2008). Unpacking 'participation': Models, meanings and practices. *Community Development Journal, 43*(3), 269–283.

Cornwall, A., & Brock, K. (2005). What do buzzwords do for development policy? A critical look at 'participation','empowerment'and 'poverty reduction'. *Third World Quarterly, 26*(7), 1043–1060.

Dahl, R. A. (1957). The concept of power. *Behavioral science, 2*(3), 201–215.

Erickson, T. (1995). Notes on design practice: Stories and prototypes as catalysts for communication. In J. M. Carroll (Ed.), *Scenario-based design* (pp. 37–58). New York: Wiley.

Freire, P. (1970). *Pedagogy of the oppressed* (Trans: M. B. Ramos). New York: Continuum.

Gaventa, J. (2006). Perspectives on participation and citizenship. In R. Mohanty & R. Tandon (Eds.), *Participatory citizenship: Identity, exclusion, inclusion* (pp. 51–67). London: Sage.

Guijt, I., & Shah, M. K. (1998). Waking up to power, conflict and process. In I. Guijt & M. K. Shah (Eds.), *The myth of community: Gender issues in participatory development* (Vol. 228–242). London: Intermediate Technology Publications.

Harder, M., Burford, G., & Hoover, E. (2013). What is participation? Design leads the way to a cross-disciplinary framework. *Design Issues, 29*(4), 41–57.

Hyysalo, S., & Lehenkari, J. (2002). *Contextualizing power in a collaborative design*. Paper presented at the PDC 2002, Malmö.

Kanstrup, A. M., & Christiansen, E. (2006). *Selecting and evoking innovators: Combining democracy and creativity*. Paper presented at the proceedings of the 4th Nordic conference on human-computer interaction: Changing roles.

Maquil, V. (2010). *The ColorTable: An interdisciplinary design process*. Wien: Vienna University of Technology.

McClelland, D. C. (1975). *Power: The inner experience*. New York: Wiley.

Pretty, J. (1995). Participatory learning for sustainable agriculture. *World Development, 23*(8), 1247–1263.

Robertson, T., & Wagner, I. (2012). Ethics: Engagement, representation and politics-in-action. In J. Simonsen & T. Robertson (Eds.), *Routledge international handbook of participatory design* (pp. 64–85). London: Routledge.

Rocha, E. M. (1967). A ladder of empowerment. *Journal of Planning Education and Research, 17*(1), 31–44.

Rodwell, C. M. (1996). An analysis of the concept of empowerment. *Journal of Advanced Nursing, 23*(2), 305–313.

Ruland, C. M., Starren, J., & Vatne, T. M. (2008). Participatory design with children in the development of a support system for patient-centered care in pediatric oncology. *Journal of Biomedical Informatics, 41*(4), 624–635.

Sending, V. A. (2006). *En kvalitativ undersøkelse av elementer som motiverer barn til å bruke et diagnostiseringssystem* (Master thesis). Oslo University.

The World Bank. (1994). *The world bank and participation*. Washington DC: Operations Policy Department.

Vatne, T. M., et al. (2013). Effects of an interactive symptom communication tool for children with heart disease on patient-provider communication in outpatient care: Preliminary results. *Journal of Communication in Healthcare, 6*(2), 106–114.

Wagner, I. (2011). Building urban narratives: Collaborative site-seeing and envisioning in the MR Tent. *Computer Supported Cooperative Work (CSCW), 21*(1), 1–42.

Wagner, I., Basile, M., Ehrenstrasser, L., Maquil, V., Terrin, J.-J., & Wagner, M. (2009). *Supporting community engagement in the city: Urban planning in the MR-tent.* Paper presented at the proceedings of the fourth international conference on communities and technologies.

Wallerstein, N., & Bernstein, E. (1994). Introduction to community empowerment, participatory education, and health. *Health Education & Behavior, 21*(2), 141–148.

White, S. C. (1996). Depoliticising development: The uses and abuses of participation. *Development in Practice, 6*(1), 6–15.

Zündorf, L. (1986). Macht, Einfluß, Vertrauen und Verständigung. Zum Problem der Handlungskoordinierung in Arbeitsorganisationen. In R. Seltz, U. Mill, & E. Hildebrandt (Eds.), *Organisation als soziales System* (pp. 33–56). Berlin: Sigma.

Chapter 8
Conclusions

In this book we have tried to disentangle the concept of participation by taking a closer look at power and decision-making—as well as on participation itself. Now it is time to look back and reflect on the concepts and how they have helped us understand the PD practices in the two projects. Let us look once more at the three concepts: power, decision-making, and participation.

8.1 Looking Back at How Power was Enacted

Power in PD is about how to get a voice and a say—what are the strategies and resources available to the participants in a PD project? We have emphasized the positive, enabling aspects of power. But we have also pointed at the constraints that result from structural aspects of power, such as: the institutional framing of a project, temporal structures, formal authority over decisions concerning budget and hiring, and so forth. Power is a 'troubling concept' and we have tried to arrive at a nuanced understanding of the different 'shades' of power, including influence, mutual understanding, trust, loyalty, as well as the impact of power/knowledge in our analysis of decision-making.

In the discussion of power issues it is often the 'power to' of particular people, which is in the foreground. The constructive 'power to' aspect captures the ability to accomplish design moves, making use of imagination and the available knowledge, even under the constraints of deadlines, limited resources and conflicting ideas. This may require exercising influence or mobilizing trust and loyalty: there are different ways the challenges of collaboration in a PD project are managed to move towards a good result.

Looking back we can say that both projects assembled different power/knowledges with their specific modes of expression: technical, domain-related, research-based, artistic, and so forth. Participatory methods and techniques did not make these different forms of expertise available to all. Trust and loyalty turned out to be rather important for decision-making. Choices were accepted even if not fully understood. Trust and loyalty helped go through phases of discouragement and conflicts.

T. Bratteteig, I. Wagner, *Disentangling Participation,* Computer Supported
Cooperative Work, DOI 10.1007/978-3-319-06163-4_8,
© Springer International Publishing Switzerland 2014

Both projects had strong project leaders who had a vision and the willingness to exercise power in the case of conflict. They also used their power to control the project resources and to hire the professional expertise they thought necessary to achieve the project aims. In both projects users' expertise was respected. The vision of the project results was deeply participatory. The design results that have been developed increased the 'power to' of users, giving a voice to citizens in urban planning and ill children in consultations with doctors.

Sisom was vision-driven, not starting from users perceiving a need. The project leader was motivated by her commitment to improving the treatment of children with cancer. She did not share her 'power over' but recruited different participants for rather narrowly defined tasks. This narrowed the scope of participation in the project. The most important participants—the children—contributed as experts on how children talk about symptoms. The project leader trusted that they would act like children but they had very limited influence, contributing to small tasks, such as organizing the vocabulary, creating ideas for how to the present symptoms and how to navigate, and, finally, accepting the professional remake of some of their ideas. Still, with their sketches, drawings and stories, the children created choices, which are visible in the design result.

IPCity was also vision-driven but more participatory. The project leader shared power with the designer team, as well as with the urban planning team: a powerful user partner. 'Normal' citizens—lay people—contributed mainly as 'testers' of the *MR-Tent*. We have seen how important this role was: as workshop participants, users contributed to the 'seeing' part of design moves, which defines the basis for the next move. They exercised 'power to' through the ways they used the relatively open technologies of the *ColorTable* to resolve controversial issues and built a vision for an urban site. They dealt actively with some of the imperfections of the *ColorTable* prototype.

The differences between the two projects are not just a result of the two project leaders having a rather different idea about how to organize the design process. One obvious difference is that while *IPCity* was a research project, *Sisom* was focused from the beginning on creating a product that would be useable at the children's cancer ward. This focus on a product acted as a constraint, limiting the design space from the beginning. *IPCity* had the luxury of being considered an exploratory-creative project with the idea of generating something novel. Another difference between the two projects had to do with the different kinds of power/knowledge represented by the medical profession in the case of *Sisom*, urban planners in the case of *IPCity*. Being 'evidence-based', combined with the commitment to 'normalising' practices, is a rather powerful 'rule' in the medical field. It made the idea of building a vocabulary bottom-up appear unprofessional. The power/knowledge of urban planners was of a different kind: how to visualize 'urban concepts' (and make them audible) was much more open to interpretation. What both projects had in common were end-users—children with cancer, 'normal' citizens—that were difficult to enrol with stable participation over time.

8.2 Looking Back at Decision-Making

According to Alfred Schütz, decisions are intricately embedded in people's practices. Choices are only opened up in situations which 'give rise to a decisive new experience: the experience of doubt, of questioning, of choosing and deciding, in short, of deliberation' (Schütz 1951, p. 169). Design moves happen when choices are created, selected, materialized in a prototype, and evaluated, thereby opening up for new choices and the next design moves. Creativity and imagination are about generating choices in design. 'Mutual learning', a key concept in PD (Bratteteig et al. 2012), captures the fact that in order to recognize a choice as good and/or novel designers and users have to collaborate in understanding its 'logic', from a design as well as a use perspective.

Our analysis has exposed some key characteristics of creating and making choices in design. The main types of linkages Langley et al. describe have been useful in uncovering dependencies that can make it difficult to simply 'undo' a particular choice or that constrain the range of available options or open up new choices (Langley et al. 1995). Moving the *ColorTable* outdoors to the site of an urban project had a 'snowballing' effect: a portable shelter—the *MR-Tent*—had to be constructed, lighting conditions had to be controlled; representations of the site had to be created and edited, that made space for interventions, ignoring natural restrictions of vistas; to name just a few. In *Sisom* the use of 'islands' as a metaphor had an 'enabling' effect, as it opened up for non-sequentiality and responded to children's love of things being playful. In *IPCity* 'stakeholder participation' had a 'cascading' effect: prompting the commitment to 'immediacy' and the search for a 'new language', shaping interface and interaction design; as well as the format of participatory workshops.

The notion of linkages also helps understand that some decisions are more influential than others. For example, contributing to a choice that turns out to have *precursive* linkages to subsequent decisions on other issues provides more 'power to' than participating in small design decisions. Some issues even tend to be 'intrinsically precursive, because of the pervasive effect they are known to have on the future context and on resource allocation' (Langley et al. 1995, p. 273). Being part of recurring decisions may indicate a power struggle, with some participants questioning a choice and bringing it back on the table. Decisions may be 'laterally linked through an integrated strategy, whether this is driven by a vision of a leadership, a formal deliberate strategic plan, or patterns that simply emerge through a process of learning' (ibid, p. 273). *Lateral* linkages cut across different issues streams; and they most evidently point to issues of 'power over'. In *Sisom* the core team took these decisions, for example between alternative navigation metaphors. In *IPCity* openness, stakeholder participation and bringing MR outdoors created a context for a number of choices, some of which were contested.

In design, choices are materialized. This not only gives power to the person who has the competence to implement a decision. It also supports a particular kind of evaluating a choice with 'seeing/observing' as a salient element. Decision-making

in design is not 'just' about reflecting and discussing: it is about practically probing a materialized choice in action. A choice may then turn out to have unforeseen
effects that are difficult to resolve, such as the tracking mechanism in *IPCity*, but
almost impossible to 'undo': for lack of resources, project time or because other,
interlinked choices have already been made.

8.3   Looking Back at Participation

Our analysis has stressed the importance of a participatory result. Even a process
with limited user participation can result in a design that increases the 'power to'
of users. We have also argued, however, that a participatory result always points to
participation in the process.

Why do we emphasize this point? The two projects we analyzed in this book cannot be considered 'perfect' examples of PD. Yet they created a new space for future
users. Discussing participation and engagement, Gaventa introduces the notion of
spaces for participation and reflects on 'how to influence the power relations that
shape the boundaries of such spaces, what is possible within them, and who may enter, with which identities, discourses and interests' (Gaventa 2005, p. 11). He makes
a distinction between closed spaces, invited spaces and claimed/created or 'third'
spaces, which are outside of the institutionalized policy arenas. Gaventa argues that

> power gained in one space, through new skills, capacity and experiences, can be used to
> enter and affect other spaces. From this perspective, the transformative potential of spaces
> for participatory governance must always be assessed in relationship to the other spaces
> which surround them'. (ibid, p. 13)

IPCity created a space (and tools) for participatory urban planning. It needed the
consent of project owners and local authorities, as well as the cooperativeness of
participants. However, in each project this space was restricted to one or, including
workshop preparations, two interventions. One could argue that this is rather limited. This depends on the perspective. From the point of view of a particular urban
project, the intervention was small; from the point of view of the urban planning
team and their peers, *IPCity* opened up a new space of possibilities, helping them
understand how to better engage 'normal' citizens by providing them with a language to express their ideas and with the chance to immediately experience them in
a mixed-media environment. The space created by *Sisom* is more permanent, since
its design result continues to be used in the children's ward. McClelland's notion of
the 'power experience' (McClelland 1975) captures this aspect of PD. It expresses
that the 'power to' of users is connected with different ways of 'feeling powerful':
having contributed to helping ill children have a voice in consultations with doctors; being able to contribute to an urban project on equal footing with experts. This
confirms that even 'modest interventions' (Heath 2007) can make a contribution to
a participatory result.

An interesting question arises: is silence a participatory action (Finken and Stue-dahl 2008; Mörtberg and Studedahl 2005)? For example, workshop participants re-jected much of the content the team had prepared for them to construct their vision. This may have different reasons. In the *IPCity* workshop in Oslo the participants preferred images and sketches of content that seemed realistic. Not only that: '...even if all participants had mentioned in the interviews that the bridge at *Blindern station* is very slippery, nobody used the content cards representing snow or ice' (Bratteteig and Wagner 2012, p. 9). Hence they silenced concerns they had stated before. In the same workshop session, the expert-participant, an architect, put a sheet of transparent paper on the physical map and sketching his solution on it. He converted the *ColorTable* using it with his customary tools. Even if a space has been created, participants have the power to not participate, to withdraw, to refuse, or to use the tool in an unexpected way. In PD the choices—'moves'—are to be 'seen' from all the perspective of all participants. Hence, silence can be interpreted as a critique that takes the form of lack of support for a certain choice, suggesting to 'move back' or 'undo' the move (Rolstad 2014). Unsupported moves often do not make it to the design result.

One of our main conclusions is that understanding participation requires a de-tailed view of decision-making in a project. We need to know where in the dynam-ics of 'see-move-see', the opening up of choices and the selection of particular choices, participation actually happens. This is not easy though. While involved in an ongoing project, a lot of process and result knowledge is needed to foresee the implications of some choices, their scope and relevance. Hence, how choices are made in a design project depends on the extent and quality of 'mutual learning': learning enough about the other position to be able to understand it while still being able to maintain one's own position. We have described how some of the conflicts in a project have to do with consequences of decisions that were not clear to all participants. This indicates that mutual learning may not have been nurtured enough for 'agonistic positions' to be clarified (Bjögvinsson et al. 2012).

8.4   The Importance of a Participatory Vision

Our analysis also points to the importance of a vision for a result to be participa-tory. We have seen that the vision in both projects did not come from the users. But the process invited them to share the vision and contribute with their imaginings. There is a 'utopian moment' associated with PD, which is about designing futures. We refer to the notion of utopia as Ernst Bloch formulated it in 'The Principle of Hope' (Bloch 1995), where he described how utopian thinking has contributed to the development of society. He made a distinction between abstract utopias that are un-embedded in reality, and concrete utopias that are grounded in the possible. To Bloch, utopia was a horizon, a place beyond reach but within view. By aspiring to it, people could become active in the production of a better world.

Reflecting on utopian thinking Hatuka and D'Hooghe point to dissent over its role in the field of architecture. While some architects have argued against utopian ideals as requiring 'totalitarian coercion and physical determinism', others maintain that ideal visions remain an essential catalyst for any kind of social development. Thus in urban design conceptions of what makes a 'Good City' must be central to both, theory and practice. This is always a challenge, as can be seen from the difficulties planners often have of reconciling 'their need to address everyday life with a wish to engage abstract concepts in pursuit of alternatives' (Hatuka and D'Hooghe 2007, p. 21).

Hatuka and D'Hooghe maintain that 'it is difficult to keep alive, however feebly, the possibility of socio-political culture without an "alternate" or utopian vision of society', adding that 'imagining (such) an alternative future is possible only by distancing oneself from the constraints of the pragmatic and the consensual' (ibid, p. 24). We agree with them that the potential paradoxes between the exigencies of everyday life and utopian thinking have to be taken seriously.

These arguments are not new to PD. Referring to the writings of Paul Ricoeur (1978), Markussen points at the intricate relationships between envisioning the future and thinking about the past:

> From a "historising" perspective, however, it is not just ideas about future work that are created and reflected in cooperative settings and other kinds of design, ideas that are meant to transcend the tradition or a given reality in the present. Vis à vis new ideas of how to work, as the prototype suggested, the given reality is also shaped in a specific way: it is not simply there in any self evident way. Hermeneutically speaking, a horizon of expectation of the future implies a certain way of thinking about the past. It interprets experiences in a distinctive way and creates a specific space of experience of the past. (Markussen 1996, p. 132)

Engaging in PD always means balancing how the past and the present are perceived within visions of the future.

Participatory projects can have different ambitions though. Is the ambition to design tools that for example help improve working conditions; or perform certain tasks faster, with more ease; or augment them so as to make them more challenging? Is it to make a tool that helps users transform their practice or even evolve new kinds of practice?

Both projects had the ambition to help establish a novel practice: giving children an active role in symptom assessment; providing 'normal' citizens with a language and a tool to raise their voice in urban planning projects. In both cases this meant increasing users' 'power to'. However, results such as these need grounding within a community or organization. In the pioneering days of PD support came from trade unions, even though these may not always have engaged as deeply as the designers expected (Clement and Van den Besselaar 1993). Today anchoring participatory results in an organization may be more difficult. In the case of *Sisom,* the fact that the project leader herself was part of the hospital's research department and that she insisted on an evidence-based approach, helped establish the project results. Most importantly, *Sisom* resulted in a tool that was easy to use and immediately available. *IPCity* produced a prototypal realization of the vision, which was far too complex to be easily turned into a product. Moreover, the *ColorTable* came with a resource-intensive method: participants have to be prepared in advance, visual and auditory content as well as panoramic views have to be produced and edited. Hence, using a participatory tool like the *ColorTable* presupposes a considerable commitment from those who plan an urban project.

8.5 Disentangling Participation

Two issues (and questions) shaped our motivation for this book. The first of these issues refers to the 'dilemma between the moral stance of PD of sharing power and the fact that designers as experts in "making" IT systems and artifacts have considerable power'. The second and related question is how participatory a design project has to be so as to 'qualify' as a PD project.

In our analysis we dealt with the power of designers that has been so eloquently argued by Finken in her study of web designers (Finken 2005). It is in the power of the designer to interpret what users voice as their needs and preferences and translate these into a design result, using his/her power/knowledge. Looking at power from the perspective of decision-making gives a more complex picture of this power. A design project involves many kinds and levels of decisions. Choices have implications, opening up for or constraining the space for other choices, affecting other choices in sometimes-unforeseen ways. This relativizes the power of designers. Moreover, 'making' is not a straightforward process. It is open to 'seeing/evaluating', probing additional choices, making the next move, and so forth. In this process more participants than the designer are involved. Hence, the designer makes the thing but this 'thing-in-the-making' is open as long as the design process lasts. While we can say that the designer makes the thing (depending on choices on many levels and of many kinds), the user 'makes' the use, appropriating the design. Coming back to the disciplining power of discourses, or in our case 'things', PD aims at resisting or undermining the normalizing effects of power (Robertson and Wagner 2012). This does not say, however, that a participatory tool is never disciplining. In *Sisom*, for example, the design result disciplines doctors in the sense of obliging them to take account of the voice of sick children. In *IPCity* the *ColorTable* helped users contest architects' power/knowledge.

Our analysis has uncovered a strong link between participation and 'power to'. We think that coming to such a conclusion requires asking: participation in what? We identified different arenas for participation in a design project: creating choices, selecting among choices, implementing or materializing a choice, seeing/evaluating, and making the next move. Users don't have to participate in all these arenas to contribute to a participatory result. We think of creating choices and seeing/evaluating as the strongest possibilities for participation. Implementing/making is the arena, in which the technical skills and competencies of designers dominate. Selecting is the point where one can see how much users' contributions, their choices and observations, are taken into account. If they can see their position represented in the participatory result, they know that they have participated.

'Participation in what?' This begs a number of questions those engaged in PD might want or should address: Did the participants create choices—or parts of choices—that were respected as valid choices in the decision-making? Did they participate in the selection of choices? Were their choices considered in the decision-making even if they were not selected? Was participants' 'seeing' considered and made part of design decisions? Did they create and or make choices that are visible in the design result? Does the design result give a (weak) participating user a stronger voice or change the power relations in the (main) use situation? Our conclusion is that PD needs to address all these questions. However, the participatory result is the most significant aspect of a design process, since this is what PD seeks to achieve.

References

Bjögvinsson, E., Ehn, P., & Hillgren, P.-A. (2012). Design things and design thinking: Contemporary participatory design challenges. *Design Issues, 28*(3), 101–116.

Bloch, E. (1995). *The principle of hope.* Cambridge: MIT Press.

Bratteteig, T., & Wagner, I. (2012). Spaces for participatory creativity. *CoDesign, 8*(2–3), 105–126.

Bratteteig, T., Bødker, K., Dittrich, Y., Mogensen, P. H., & Simonsen, J. (2012). Methods: Organising principles and general guidelines for participatory design projects. In J. Simonsen & T. Robertson (Eds.), *Routledge international handbook of participatory design* (pp. 177–144). London: Routledge.

Clement, A., & Van den Besselaar, P. (1993). A retrospective look at PD projects. *Communications of the ACM, 36*(6), 29–37.

Finken, S. (2005). *Methods as technologies for producing knowledge. An encounter with cultural practices—reflections from a field study in a high-tech company.* (PhD), Roskilde University, Roskilde.

Finken, S., & Stuedahl, D. (2008). *Silence' as an analytical category for PD.* Paper presented at the proceedings of the tenth anniversary conference on participatory design, Indiana University.

Gaventa, J. (2005). *Reflections on the uses of the 'Power Cube' approach for analyzing the spaces, places and dynamics of civil society participation and engagement CFP evaluation series 2003–2006* (p. 46). Brighton: University of Sussex.

Hatuka, T., & D'Hooghe, A. (2007). After postmodernism: Readdressing the role of Utopia in urban design and planning. *Places, 19*(2), 20–27.

Heath, D. (2007). Bodies, antibodies and modest interventions. In K. Asdal, B. Brenna, & I. Moser (Eds.), *Technoscience: The politics of interventions* (pp. 135–156). Oslo: Oslo Academic Press.

Langley, A., Mintzberg, H., Pitcher, P., Posada, E., & Saint-Macary, J. (1995). Opening up decision-making. *Organization Science, 6*(3), 260–279.

Markussen, R. (1996). Politics of intervention in design: Feminist reflections on the Scandinavian tradition. *AI & Society, 10,* 127–141.

McClelland, D. C. (1975). *Power: The inner experience.* New York: Wiley.

Mörtberg, C., & Studedahl, D. (2005). *Silences and sensibilities: Increasing participation in IT design.* Paper presented at the proceedings of the 4th decennial conference on critical computing: Between sense and sensibility, Aarhus.

Ricoeur, P. (1978). The metaphorical process as cognition, imagination, and feeling. *Critical Inquiry, 5*(1), 143–159.

Robertson, T., & Wagner, I. (2012). Ethics: Engagement, representation and politics-in-action. In J. Simonsen & T. Robertson (Eds.), *Routledge international handbook of participatory design* (pp. 64–85). London: Routledge.

Rolstad, O. K. (2014). *The life and death of design ideas* (Master thesis). Oslo: University of Oslo.

Schütz, A. (1951). Choosing among projects of action. *Philosophy and Phenomenological Research, 12*(2), 161–184.

Printed in the United States
By Bookmasters